THE PUZZLE OF EVIL

Books by Peter Vardy
available from M.E. Sharpe

THE PUZZLE OF ETHICS
(with Paul Grosch)

THE PUZZLE OF GOD

THE PUZZLE OF THE GOSPELS
(with Mary Mills)

The Puzzle of Evil

PETER VARDY

M.E. Sharpe
Armonk, New York
London, England

First U.S. edition, 1997.
Published in the U.S. by M. E. Sharpe, Inc.

Copyright © 1992 by Peter Vardy
First published in Great Britain in 1992 by Fount Paperbacks

Library of Congress Cataloging-in-Publication Data

Vardy, Peter.
The puzzle of evil / Peter Vardy.
p.   cm.
Originally published: London : Fount, 1992.
ISBN 0-7656-0167-2 (hardcover : alk. paper). —
ISBN 0-7656-0168-0 (pbk. : alk. paper)
1. Good and evil.   2. Theodicy.   I. Title.
BJ1401.V37   1997
214—dc21   97-2910
CIP
Printed in the United States of America

The paper used in this publication meets the minimum requirements of
American National Standard for Information Sciences—
Permanence of Paper for Printed Library Materials,
ANSI Z 39.48-1984.

BM (c)   10   9   8   7   6   5   4   3   2   1
BM (p)   10   9   8   7   6   5   4   3   2   1

TO MY FAMILY –

*My wife Anne and our children
Catherine, Christian, Leah, Luke and Kirsten.*

*With my thanks for
their patience and love.*

CONTENTS

LETTER TO THE READER

Dear Reader,

Come with me on a quest, an adventure. Like any quest it involves a search but in this case our quest is for unseen realities. We will probe the existence and nature of those dark and evil forces that seem to torment human beings and will try, as we go, to understand how it can possibly be that these fearsome forces exist in a world which many hold has been created by a wholly good and all-powerful God. This is no search for fairies, no hunt for a snark, no myth to entertain during idle hours, but a search for truth and understanding about the ultimate nature of evil.

We all have to die, we all have to face mental and physical pain, yet most of us know that the suffering of others is far worse than anything we shall ever experience. Our television screens make us recoil in horror from pictures of the death camps, of people starving to death in Africa or children who have been beaten and abused by their own parents. How can we make sense of it all? This book is intended to help you to answer this question for yourself. It is in two parts – the first covers reasonably well-trodden ground and takes up about a third of the book. It explains how thinkers before us have tackled these issues and what the strengths and weaknesses of their approaches are. In the second part, I try to find a new path, a new way of understanding the old problems, and invite you to accompany me on the journey.

Many people have helped me directly and indirectly in writing this book. My postgraduate and undergraduate students at Heythrop College, University of London, where I lecture in philosophy of religion have made a real contribution to the first part with their

The Puzzle of Evil

enthusiasm and questions as we probed these issues together. In particular I would record my thanks to Vic Coughtrey and Rory Fox. Others, however, have helped me by the example of their own journeys and their friendship. I am particularly grateful to Sr Carmelina, a now retired Dominican Sister in South Africa, who taught my wife when she was at school; to Sr Anne-Marie Quigg who by her friendship as well as her work and example in Africa have helped me understand a great deal; to Fr Michael Ruddy of Ireland for his honesty and openness; to the Revd Gordon Dowden who has devoted his life to the people of inner-city Manchester; to the Revd Robert Corbin, the former vicar of Selborne in Hampshire where I lived for ten happy years; to George Wilde S.J. of Heythrop College who died in the week this book went to the printers and whose gentleness and faith I will long remember; and to the Revd Nigel Mead of Shebbear in Devon whose kindness and patient example have been an inspiration. Above all my thanks are due to Anne, my wife of eighteen very happy years, for her constant love and support.

PETER VARDY

Heythrop College
University of London
Pentecost 1991 to Epiphany 1992

St Clair
Devon, England

PART I

THE PROBLEM OF EVIL

Is God willing to prevent evil, but not able? Then he is impotent. Is he able but not willing? Then he is malevolent. Is he both able and willing? Whence then is evil?

EPICURUS

ONE

The Problem Stated

> Why is there any misery in the world? Not by chance, surely. From some cause then. Is it then from the intention of the deity? But he is perfectly benevolent. Is it contrary to his intention? But he is almighty. Nothing can shake the solidity of this reasoning. So short, so clear, so decisive . . .
>
> DAVID HUME, *Dialogues concerning Natural Religion*, Penguin, pp.III–I2

Try to think of someone who is really evil. Many people would immediately pick on Hitler yet even Hitler had many good points. Hitler's leadership and his party transformed a war-torn and ravaged Germany, which had been bled dry by the Allied powers after the First World War, into a modern and prosperous nation. Hitler loved children and was faithful to his friends. Of course, the slaughter of the Jews, gypsies, Poles and others as well as the expansionist policies which led to the Second World War were malevolently evil, but the issue is more complicated than may at first appear. The Spanish dictator Franco was vilified by most of the Western and Eastern world, but his officials saved more Jews in the Second World War than did the French government under Pétain and he brought constitutional democracy and stability back to Spain. England celebrates the killing of Guy Fawkes, yet he was trying to get rid of a perverted king and a parliament that was hopelessly intolerant. Does that make him a terrorist fiend or simply part of the leadership of a strong opposition driven to take extreme measures to defend liberty? Oliver Cromwell, who brought democracy to England, was in many ways an ill-mannered murderer, and General Sherman's treatment of the State of Georgia in the Civil War was unforgiveable in its ferocity. Almost always black is mixed with white, or at the least grey.

What is evil? It is too easy to think that suffering and evil are the same, but are they? An inoculation may be painful, but it is good for you. An operation may cure a disease or a defect in one's body, even though pain and inconvenience may be the short-term result. Some human suffering can ennoble the individual, although it must be recognized that it can destroy as well. One needs to relate the eventual good to the assumed evil.

If the problem of evil is to be considered fully then it must necessarily be discussed in relation to God. The existence of God and the reality of evil have always been closely interrelated issues. As a first step the assumptions on which the whole debate about evil rests need to be examined. The presence of evil is unquestioned, but if there is a good God how can it be explained?

Many attempts have been made to solve this problem. Classically, there have been two different approaches:

1. *The Irenean Tradition* develops a theodicy which accepts God's partial responsibility for evil. Ireneus (a.d. 130–202) attempts to show the good reasons which made the existence of evil inevitable. He claims that human beings were created as imperfect creatures who had to be brought to perfection by development and growth. Evil was a means to this end. The world with its mingled good and evil is, for Ireneus, part of God's plan and purpose. Ireneus gives little place to any idea of a fall from perfection and explains evil by looking forward to what is achieved as a result of its presence in the universe. Humans, therefore, have responsibility for evil but are not solely responsible. Clement of Alexandria (who died in a.d. 220, soon after Ireneus), largely shared his view by holding that human beings were created immature and had to grow to goodness.

2. *The Augustinian Tradition* sought to entirely remove responsibility for the existence of evil from God by blaming it on dependent beings who have, by their own free decision, misused the gift of freedom that God has given them. God is not to blame for evil as all blame can be laid at the door of human beings and fallen angels. For Augustine, the world was originally created perfect and fell from this state through the exercise of free will and contrary to God's intention. Augustine was strongly influenced by Plato and, in his approach, the personality and love of God are not central.

These two approaches are different but, in spite of their differences, they share a number of assumptions which appear so obvious that they are sometimes not recognized.

Opening assumptions

Either this world was created by God or it was not. If it was not, then the universe must have always existed. Demonstrating this is straightforward:

> Assume that at one time there was nothing. It is clear that nothing can come from nothing. If, therefore, there was once nothing, even now there would be nothing. The universe cannot, therefore, have come into existence from nothing unless something brought it into existence.
>
> However, we know that the universe now exists. If God, or something equivalent in terms of power, does not exist then the universe must always have existed since, if it was not created, it could not have come into existence of its own accord from nothing. (This is a paraphrase of part of an argument from St Thomas Aquinas' Third Way of proving the existence of God.)

The standard theory of the creation of the universe is that there was an original explosion, the Big Bang, which took place about 15 billion years ago. Since this initial explosion the universe has been expanding outwards. The explosive force of the expansion is, however, counteracted by the force of gravitation which strives to contract the universe. There is a very fine balance between these two forces. If the strength of the Big Bang had been just a little bit larger (1/10 to the power of 60 – an incredibly tiny amount), then matter would have been thrown out at such a speed that there would have been no chance for galaxies to be formed. If, however, the strength of the Big Bang had been the same amount less, then the force of gravity would have caused the universe to collapse in on itself.

Scientists are fairly clear about how the universe developed from the first hundred thousandth of a second onwards – what happened in this first infinitesimal period is, however, still unknown. We do know that galaxies and their stars are getting further and further apart all the time. There are two basic possibilities in the future. Either this expansion process will continue or, at some stage, the rate of expansion will slow and the galaxies will start to fall in on themselves again.

The Big Bang theory need not necessarily point to God. Possibly there was a continual series of universes that have existed, each starting from its own Big Bang, each expanding over unimaginable distance and time and each collapsing once more – before another Big Bang started the whole process again.

The claim that the universe is everlasting, that in some form or other it has always and will always exist is, therefore, not impossible. It cannot be proved to be false and the atheist or humanist will maintain this position.

The *theist* is the person who believes in a single God who is an incorporeal agent – i.e. who can act in the universe that he has created. Theists are generally Christians, Jews or Muslims and will claim that the universe was created by God. This God, they will hold, necessarily exists – he could not fail to exist. The universe was not only created by this God but is sustained or kept in existence by this same God. This is a perfectly reasonable theory which is held by hundreds of millions of people around the world but there is a difference of opinion as to whether it can be proved to be true. Aquinas and modern supporters such as Brian Davies think that such a proof is possible, others maintain that all the proofs rest on assumptions which cannot be justified.

In this book we shall be concerned with the second of these two views, with the claim that the universe was created by God. The alternative view is credible, however, and we must recognize that our discussion starts with an unproved assumption – the existence of a single creator God.

If someone believes in two Gods, one of whom is good and the other of whom is evil, then this entails a *Cosmic Dualism* – the belief that there are two equal and opposed forces existing in the universe. On this basis, the evil that exists is to be expected as it is due to the action of an evil power which the good power is battling to overcome. Theism, however, maintains that there is a single God and rejects cosmic dualism – although we shall have to return to examine its persuasiveness later.

The assumption that there is a single God is not the only one made when discussing the problem of evil. The theist does not just hold that a single God created the universe. He or she also maintains that this God continues to be interested in the universe. This view may be rejected. The *deist* holds that God did, indeed, create the universe but has left it and is not interested in its progress or development. The theist rejects this view.

When starting to consider the reality of evil in the world, we have, therefore, two initial assumptions:

1. A single God exists who created the universe from nothing,
2. This God continues to be interested in his creation.

These are major premises and many will not accept them. However, unless these two assumptions are accepted, there is no problem of evil to worry about. The philosophic problem arises because of the difficulty of reconciling God's creation, his care for his creation and the evil we find in the world.

God's care for his creation must, however, be a benevolent care. God must be good if the problem of evil is to arise. If God was in some sense evil, if he enjoyed the sufferings of Auschwitz or the pain that many humans inflict on others, then it is not surprising that we have a world in which this type of suffering so often occurs. The theist maintains, however, that God is wholly, perfectly good and, indeed, the source of all goodness and that he is *Omnipotent* – God can do anything. God's goodness is not, therefore, limited by his inability to act.

We cannot, of course, fully understand what it means for God to be good, but it must mean at least as much and a great deal more than it does for humans to be good – God is, after all, meant to be the source of all goodness. In particular, theists maintain that God does not wish human suffering on earth to take place (in the case of animal suffering, theists tend to be more divided as we shall see later).

We have, therefore, five basic assumptions to start with:

1. A single God exists who created the universe from nothing,
2. This God continues to be interested in his creation,
3. God is good,
4. God is omnipotent,
5. God does not wish suffering to take place.

If we are willing to give up one of these assumptions, then evil is no longer a problem.

- If the universe is simply a brute fact that has always existed then the nature of the universe is not due to any agent or God. The world is as it is and we must live in it, we must make the best of it. We have no alternative!
- If God is no longer interested in his creation, then evil can be explained as being due to divine neglect.

- If God is not good then evil may be directly due to God's will.
- If God is not omnipotent, then God may not have had the power to prevent evil, for instance if there is a cosmic power for good and an equal cosmic power for evil, then evil may be simply explained by the action of the evil power.
- If evil is held not to exist or to exist only in the minds of human beings, then there is no problem that needs to be resolved.

If we reason simply from the facts in the world as we perceive them, David Hume and John Stuart Mill argue that there is no way that we can arrive at the existence of an all-powerful and wholly good God. (See Mill's *Three Essays on Religion* and Hume's *Dialogues concerning Natural Religion*.) Both these philosophers looked at the traditional forms of the design argument for the existence of God and took seriously the evil to be found in the world. To both of them, this evil seemed to be unnecessary and avoidable if God really created the world from nothing. They therefore argued that *either* God must not be wholly good so that he was not concerned with human suffering *or* that he was lacking in power and therefore not omnipotent (their arguments are outlined in my book *The Puzzle of God*, HarperCollinsFlame, 1990).

At the outset, therefore, we need to recognize that evil is only a problem if we make some fairly major assumptions. For the Christian, the Jew or the Muslim, evil and suffering are, indeed, a very real problem – for those who reject belief in God there may well be puzzlement as to what the problem is, although they may still be bewildered by the depths to which human beings can sink and the agony they can and do inflict on each other.

In this book, we will be examining the nature of the problem of evil, trying to understand how it has been dealt with and seeking to determine whether the criticisms of them are so strong that belief in the traditional understanding of God should be rejected. Many today take this view and, as we shall see, they have good arguments on their side. The question we must discuss is whether the arguments are compelling. One of the aims of this book is to set out the argument to help you, the reader, to make your own decision and to think through just what the presence of evil means for you.

TWO

A God's Eye View

> I repeat the question. Is the world, considered in general,
> and as it appears to us in this life, different from what a
> man or such a limited being would, beforehand, expect
> from a very wise, powerful and benevolent deity?
>
> D A V I D H U M E , *Dialogues concerning*
> *Natural Religion*, Penguin, p.115

The problem of evil is very obvious when we look at the world
from our point of view, from an anthropomorphic perspective. There
is, however, an alternative to this and that is to take a theocentric
approach or a God's-eye view to reality. The approach to the problem
of evil taken by St Augustine of Hippo (a.d. 354–430) and St Thomas
Aquinas (a.d. 1226–1274) follows this line.

Augustine, in *The City of God*, had faced the problem of combining
the personal God of the Bible with the ideas of the Ultimate, the
Perfect, the Immutable which had been put forward by Greek
philosophy. He held that God is beyond time and space, absolutely
immutable, in other words God is completely unchangeable and
cannot be other than God is. Aquinas followed this view and argued
that whilst language about God may be true, it cannot have the same
meaning as when it is applied to human beings or other parts of
the created order. Aquinas therefore rejects both univocal and
straightforwardly equivocal language when applied to God and instead
maintains that we can talk abut God only through analogy and
metaphor.

Aquinas' formulation of the problem of evil is precise. He
recognizes that if one of two opposing forces is infinite the other

The Puzzle of Evil

must be excluded absolutely. God, however, is infinitely good and is all-powerful. How, then, can there be any evil?

Given that Aquinas recognized the problem so clearly, it is to be expected that his solution would be equally clear – and this is, indeed, the case. The Thomist approach to the problem of evil has become normative within the Roman Catholic tradition and it must be taken seriously because of its depth and profundity. The primary philosophic influence on Aquinas was Aristotle, whose writings had been rediscovered in the West shortly before Aquinas' time, having been preserved by Islamic scholars.

Aristotle maintained that in any pair of contraries, one is always negative in relation to the other – thus dark is an absence of light; poverty is an absence of wealth and evil is an absence of good (his technical way of putting this was to say that there was an antithesis between fullness or completion ("*habitus*") and lack of it ("*privatio*")).

Augustine adopted this distinction, with amendments. He held that good was a substance which was ultimately most fully expressed in God. Evil, on the other hand, was not a substance at all, it was "no substance, but the perversion of the will, turned aside from God" (Confessions VII, 22), in other words evil does not exist as a thing but represents our willing things opposed to God. For Augustine, therefore, moral evil represented a privation or lack ("*privatio boni*" or privation of the good) whilst natural evil could also be seen as a privation as well as being a punishment for sin or a necessary part of the overall system.

Augustine wrote partly to answer the Manichaeans (who were founded by Mani (a.d. 215–276)) and who maintained a metaphysical dualism – saying that there were equal evil and good powers at work in the universe. Augustine rejected this, claiming that all substances are good because God created them. Any corruption of these substances cannot come from God. Augustine declared thorns and thistles and even the flames of hell to be good. The Manichaeans replied that anyone who thought this should try putting a scorpion on his hand. Augustine countered saying that even poison was good in itself and good for the scorpion (Morals of the Manichaeans. 8.11). Even the Manichaeans' idea of a kingdom of evil had in it things that were good in themselves such as power, memory, life and intelligence. Augustine concluded:

> All these things . . . cannot be called evil: for all such things, as far as they exist, must have their existence from the most high God, for as far as they exist they are good.
>
> (Morals of the Manichaeans 9.14)

Aquinas was strongly influenced by Augustine's interpretation in this area and his approach can be summarized as follows:

1. In the Summa Theologiae 1a, 48 (hereinafter ST), Aquinas concludes that the word "evil" does not signify any essence, form or substance. Therefore it can only mean "some sort of absence of goodness". Aquinas arrives at this conclusion by assuming that all things strive for perfection and that perfection means ultimate goodness. Goodness must, therefore, be something definite otherwise one could not strive towards it and evil is not a thing but the extent to which something falls short of perfection.

Evil is the privation of good. In other words, evil is the absence of good in something which would, by the nature of what it is, be expected to have this good. We do not expect a rock to have the good of sight, if a rock cannot see it is still a perfectly good rock, similarly the absence of wings from a human being does not make him any the less good a human being. It is not part of the essential nature of what it is to be a rock or a man that they should have respectively eyes or the ability to fly. Aquinas puts it like this:

> Evil denotes the absence of good. But it is not every absence of good that is called evil. For absence of good can be understood either in a privative sense or in a purely negative sense. And absence of good in the latter sense is not evil . . . Otherwise it

would follow that a thing is evil if it lacks the good which belongs to something else. For instance, man would be evil because he lacks the swiftness of a wild goat or the strength of a lion. It is absence of good in the privative sense which is called evil.

(ST, 1a, 5, 48, 3)

So we need to distinguish:

a) *Absence*. Every finite thing will have some features that are absent from it, but where the absence does not affect the essential nature of what it is to be that thing. For instance a bird does not have eight legs like an octopus and nor does an octopus have wings like a bird. It is not part of the nature of a bird to have eight legs nor part of the nature of an octopus to have wings.

b) *Privation*. A bird is made to fly. If it does not have wings, then an essential part of what it is to be a bird, an essential part of its nature, will be missing. Privation is of some perfection which is included in the essential nature of the thing in question. It is part of the essential nature of a human being that he or she should be able to see, to hear, to talk, to walk, to communicate and to think. If, therefore, any of these are absent, this will be an evil as it will be an absence of something intrinsic to what it is to be a human being; it will be an absence of a perfection usually associated with humanity.

This division, between (a) absence or negation and (b) privation, can be applied to everything in the created order. On this analysis, a cancer tumour may be a good cancer tumour in that it performs as a cancer should perform. The evil consists in the *privation of health* which the tumour brings about. Evil is thus a by-product representing the absence of good (De Potentia 3, 6, ad 3).

2. This idea of privation is not an unjustified premise as, Aquinas holds, it is based on reason and experience as well as the failure of

any other account to explain the facts. Evil cannot be a thing, since God created all things and this would mean that God created evil. Everything God created must, as such, be good because it is made by God.

3. Anything that departs from its "being", that is not fully what it should be, is to that extent evil. To talk of evil is, in fact, to affirm the possibility of non-being; it is a recognition that things in this world fall short of what they are intended to be. In ST 1a, 48, 2, Aquinas maintains that there have to be things that are corruptible or capable of imperfection if there is to be a dynamic universe. If this was not the case, the universe would be static and thus would lack perfection.

4. Evil can occur to a greater or lesser degree to the extent that any individual deviates more or less from being fully in accordance with his/her/its intended nature. A man, therefore, who does not fulfil the nature that God has intended for him is to that extent evil.

5. Moral evil is, therefore, due to a deliberate act of human beings, who have free will, choosing to be less than God intended them to be. We are all evil in so far as we fail to live up to the true nature that God intended us to have. However, part of this nature is that we have free will, so we can choose to be less than we might be; less than God intended us to be.

6. All beings, other than God, are *Contingent*. They are "might-not-have-beens". This not only means that they might not have existed in the first place, but it also means that they can fall short of their true nature. Only God, being timeless, immutable and necessary, cannot be other than he is. Only God is totally perfect as he is fully whatever it is to be God and cannot be other than this. God is perfectly God, unlike men and women who are not perfect as they fail to be fully what God intended them to be.

7. Evil, therefore, is a necessary consequence of creation. However, nothing is wholly evil, as to exist at all is good. Anything that exists is good to the extent that it exists. It is only evil to the extent that it falls short of its true nature.

Nothing that is wholly evil can exist. Evil, as we have seen, is a privation of good, it is a falling short from a thing's true nature. Something that fell short of its true nature by 100 per cent would not exist at all. It follows, therefore, that pure evil is literally nothing at all – it simply does not exist. Aquinas considered that even Satan is good in so far as he exists and cannot be regarded as wholly evil. Satan is a creature of God and is ultimately dependent on God like any other creature. Aquinas specifically excludes, therefore, any evil power in the universe which is independent to or equal to God – he thus mirrors Augustine's rejection of the Manichaean heresy. Satan continues to exist because God allows him to do so.

8. The fact that God only created contingent beings does not mean that his omnipotence is limited. There are two main possible views of omnipotence (the most adequate definition is keenly debated):

a) Aquinas says that God is omnipotent because "he can do everything that is absolutely possible". By this, however, he does not mean anything at all, some things are not possible. Aquinas unpacks his definition by saying that "everything that does not imply a contradiction is among those possibilities in respect of which God is called omnipotent" and elucidates this by "whatever implies contradiction does not come within the scope of divine omnipotence because it cannot have the aspect of possibility. Therefore it is more appropriate to say that things cannot be done rather than that God cannot do them." (ST 1a, 25)

On this definition, God can do everything that it is really possible for God to do, given God's nature, and we find what is really possible by using the test of asking whether it is logically possible. On this view to talk of God's omnipotence being limited because God cannot draw a square circle is nonsense simply because the idea of a square circle is nonsense. Similarly, to talk of God committing suicide is impossible as God, being timeless and immutable, *cannot* (logically) be other than God is. It is, therefore, a logical impossibility for God to cease to exist.

b) God can do absolutely everything – including the logically impossible. On this view, put forward by Descartes, God can even act against logic. He could cease to exist or make square circles.

We shall return to the split between these two views later in this book. For the moment it is enough to recognize that Aquinas takes the first option. It follows that if God is to create contingent beings, it necessarily follows from this that these contingent beings have the ability to defect, or fall short. They have the ability to be less than fully what they are intended to be. If this was not possible, then the beings would not be contingent but necessary.

9. God is good because God is perfect. For Aquinas, something is good if it is fully in accordance with its nature. God is completely good as God cannot be other than he is and, therefore, is fully in accordance with his nature. It is impossible for God to be evil given the way that Aquinas has defined evil – to be evil, something must fall short of its true nature and God cannot, logically, fall short of what it is to be God since God is wholly immutable.

God has brought things into existence so that God's goodness is manifested. If God had made only one type of thing, for instance only necessary beings which could not be other than as they were created, this would imperfectly mirror God's goodness. What God has, therefore, done is to make a universe consisting of nearly unlimited numbers and types of beings (Augustine terms this the "Principle of Plenitude"). Everything in the universe fulfils the function of mirroring God.

If there is to be a range or hierarchy of created goods, some things must be less good than others. Part of this hierarchy involves having some beings that can defect from being; it involves having some created things that can be less than fully whatever God created them to be. If this was not the case, there could not be a full range of creation. If there was no corruptible good, then nothing would corrupt. The many goods manifested by change would not be present; for instance there would be no fading rose, no spring and no autumn: No birth, no marriage and no death.

God is like an artist who paints creation on a broad canvas. If the whole painting is examined, it is seen to be good – even though there may be dark and light parts in specific areas. The totality is perfect and we, as humans, err in isolating small sections of the canvas and calling these bits "unnecessary" or "pointless" evil.

10. God is responsible for natural evil in that natural evil is part of the outworking of God's perfect creation. In ST Q. 1a, 49, 1 & 2, Aquinas argues that natural evil can be traced to the agency of God but this does not apply to moral evil. However, God does not cause natural evil directly, God only causes natural evil incidentally ("*per accidens*"), for instance when a cancer growth causes great pain in the subject it just happens to be in when it is itself acting according to its nature.

Natural evils only appear to be evil when seen from our perspective. In fact they are not when looked at from God's perspective. They are the natural outworkings of creation and the whole of creation, seen from God's perspective, is perfectly good. From a human perspective we might wish some things otherwise, but this is because of our limited vision. The rabbit that is eaten by the fox might wish this could be otherwise, but this is because the rabbit adopts a lapidocentric view of the world. Seen on a broader view, the pastoral scene of which rabbit and fox are part can be seen to be very good, so it is with individual natural evils.

11. On Aquinas' view, God is not a moral agent. God is the source of all goodness. Not only is there no separate standard against which God can be measured, but God also has no moral obligations to the creatures that he creates. God has absolute rights over us – the rights of creator and owner. We, by contrast, have no rights over God. It remains, therefore, for us to be grateful for our creation and we cannot claim any rights against God.

Brian Davies, in articles in *New Blackfriars* entitled "The Problem of evil and modern philosophy" (1982 & 1983) gives an example which he claims illustrates God's goodness. A baker makes bread and he deliberately makes good bread. The goodness of the bread lies in the perfection it achieves. Its perfection, the goal of the bread, lies first in the baker and only secondarily in the bread. The baker is not a good loaf of bread, he is not, for example, described as "crusty" or "tasty". But the loaf is there by virtue of him and in being good bread it reproduces the goal conceived by the baker.

Similarly God is not a good man or a good anything else in the created world, and yet, as Creator, all goodness pre-exists in God since the whole of creation mirrors the intentions of God. As Aquinas puts it:

> God is the primary operative cause of everything, goodness and desirability fittingly belong to him ... In desiring its own perfection everything is desiring God himself, for the perfection of all things somehow resembles divine existence.

(ST 1a, 6, 1)

God's intending to create the natures of everything he creates is not something separable from Him. God is not an agent, God is not a personal spirit who has intentions or who acts. On the Thomist view, timeless God is utterly unchanging and God's actions and intentions are not separable from God's very self. This is the classical doctrine of divine simplicity which is such an important part of

Thomist thought – *God is what God does*. God is pure actuality – *not* an agent who acts.

On this basis, it has to be accepted that we cannot understand what God's goodness amounts to. This, Davies claims, is true. He maintains that there is no way of understanding what God's goodness amounts to unless we understand what God is and this is in principle impossible. When we talk of God as good, we can only do so analogously. It is true that God is good and we are right to use this term of God, but what it means we cannot know.

It is important to recognize that Aquinas is saying that human beings, just as cats, dogs, oak trees, trout and angels, all have their own natures. The nature of what it is to be a cat, a dog or a human being is generic – cats belong to the whole race of cats, dogs to the race of dogs and human beings to the race of human beings. Aquinas is not, therefore, working on the assumption that we each have an individual nature, all human beings share a common nature and each of us, as individuals, are evil to the extent that we fall short of this nature. To the extent, therefore, that we are less than perfectly what God intended us to be as human beings, we are evil. As none of us live up to Aquinas' vision of what it is to be a perfect human being, we are all, necessarily, evil.

Human beings fall short of their true nature, they "defect from being", because of the exercise of their free will. God leaves us free to respond or not, to live up to or not to live up to the possibilities inherent in our essential nature as spiritual creatures, made for fellowship with God. If we choose not to meet this standard, not to actualize this possibility, then that is our choice and it gives rise to moral evil. If we have physical defects then these will also be evils – although in this case they will have no moral connotations.

On Aquinas' view, although God is directly responsible for what appears to us, from our limited perspective, to be natural evils, God is not similarly responsible for moral evils since these result from the free choices of human beings.

Aquinas' approach is profound and has great strength. It would not have survived so long and become so influential if this was not the case. However, it can be challenged at various points. The most important ones are:

1. Aquinas assumes that all things strive for their own perfection which is reasonable. However, he also considers that perfection and ultimate goodness are equivalent. These views may be questioned. Goodness becomes a metaphysical idea of completeness rather than having any moral content and many people would want to hold that God is good in a moral sense which is not possible on the Thomist model.

2. It is not clear that human beings, as a group, have a single nature. Instead it may be held that as we are individuals, we each have our own nature. Some medical studies have held, for instance, that homosexuality is due to the genetic make-up of the individuals concerned. Biologically some people are so constituted that they are physically attracted to members of the same sex rather than to partners of the opposite sex. Clearly, no individual can control his or her own biological make-up. If, therefore, our natures are individually determined by our DNA, the genetic structures implanted in us at birth, then it may be argued that we should act in accordance with this nature (although anyone so arguing might be accused of determinism as they may be held to argue that one's nature determines one's actions). To do otherwise would be "unnatural", it would be to act against what is essential to our individual natures.

Aquinas might reply to this that homosexuality, if it is due to genetic factors, is due to faulty genetic material and it is to that extent an evil as human beings who have these genes are other than God intended for human beings. Also, of course, the fact that our genes may incline us in a particular direction does not mean that we have to actualize this tendency.

3. Even if there is such a thing as a single human nature, it is far from clear what this is. For instance, part of being a human being

may well be that we have a sexual nature, we are attracted to others (even if we exclude homosexuality, the heterosexual attraction is still there) and this is an important part of our humanity. As sexual beings, we have to reproduce to maintain the population and to produce more human individuals. If we do have a sexual nature, then to deny this nature by, for instance, taking a vow of chastity may be held to be to deny an essential feature of our humanity. Opinions may well vary about what our human nature is and there seems no strong case for accepting Aquinas' view rather than alternatives put forward, for instance, by modern psychotherapists.

4. Surely there is more evil than is necessary on this view? Could not our nervous system, for instance, have been better designed to minimize pain? What benefit is there in the pain of childbirth?

A quantitative judgement is being made here and these are the hardest judgements of all to make as there are no sound philosophic grounds for making them. Such judgements are very much an individual matter. However, anyone who has seen the pain of a child of five dying in agony from throat cancer or the suffering of a woman with advanced cancer of the intestine slowly dying while her children watch may have questions to ask about the benevolence of the God who is ultimately responsible. Aquinas would consider that the levels of pain allowed are acceptable and, indeed, that the good God must have created a good nervous system. However, this is exactly the sort of move that can be challenged – one might argue the other way round (as David Hume does) and maintain that a poorly designed human body points to a limited God.

We can see here the problem of very different perspectives. Aquinas looks at the problem of evil from a theocentric perspective and is highly persuasive if his viewpoint and the resultant definitions are accepted, whereas others may reject this perspective entirely.

5. In Aquinas' time, people thought that God created different things and different species of animals and plants directly. We now know,

since Darwin, that these differences were due to evolution. Some modification to Aquinas' basic ideas would, therefore, be needed to see God as bringing about the hierarchy of creation through the process of natural selection. There seems no problem with this, provided that the suffering of animals and men over tens of thousands of years can be contemplated with equanimity. Aquinas shows no concern over suffering in the natural order and today many would consider this position to be unacceptable.

6. Aquinas' approach, starting from a theocentric perspective and from a definition of God's goodness, argues that all of creation is good and natural evils only appear to be evils to us. It is very important to recognize that when Aquinas uses "good" and "perfect" he is not using these terms in a moral sense. What it means for God to be good depends on God's nature and since God's nature is unknown to us we cannot know what it means to talk of God as being good (see Davies' example of the baker above).

Nevertheless we are sentient beings whom God is held to love, and natural evils do not just appear to be evils from our point of view, they *are* evils. It may not be easy to define evil precisely, but to those whose homes are engulfed by a freak tidal wave or who are killed by a volcano unexpectedly erupting these are real evils – even though they may be the outworking of natural forces which in other circumstances may well be good. Possibly from God's perspective, the creation was indeed good, but from man's point of view it could have been better and, if God does indeed love us, it could be argued that our point of view should have weight.

In reply, it might be argued that, as creator and owner, God has rights that go beyond any human rights. God is not a being amongst other beings. God is rather that on which all creation depends, God is the cause and sustainer of everything there is. On this view, it is a mistake to regard God as in any sense a moral agent or being, as to do so makes him too much like his creatures. Given that God created from nothing, there can be no moral obligations when nothing at all exists.

This is a possible response, but it must be questioned whether it is an adequate one. It treats God as a power source with rights over us but not obligations in return and this is a picture which we do not have to accept, particularly if God is indeed a God of love. It may be argued that *if* God creates, this does not free him from the obligation to create in the best way possible for his creatures. Aquinas' reply would be that God creates what is best for *all* his creation – our mistake is to look on things only from a human perspective. Many would argue with this – particularly if the suffering of animals over millions of years is taken into account.

7. It must be accepted on Aquinas' view that God created the universe and timelessly knew of the evils that would occur in the universe. Should God have done so given the suffering that God knew would result ? There is no simple answer to this and it is an issue to which we must return. St Bonaventure said that if one were to ask why God did not make a better world, no answer would be possible, except that God so willed it. Aquinas has no better solution to offer and his approach is vulnerable at this point. In ST 25 Aquinas says that God could have created other worlds and Aquinas is vulnerable on the point of why God chose to create *this* world. David Hume and John Mill certainly would not accept this and instead maintain that from the limitations we see in the world around us we can only conclude that God must be limited in power or in his benevolence towards his creatures.

I have real doubts as to whether Aquinas' God *could* have created other worlds – if this was possible, God would have had to have potential to choose between different courses of action and Aquinas specifically says that since God is literally timeless God has no potential. God is pure actuality rather than a being who has the potential to act in different ways. If God has no potential, there would appear to be no way in which he could choose between alternatives.

8. Finally there are wider questions as to whether a totally immutable, totally unchanging timeless and spaceless God is religiously adequate. There are serious questions as to whether such a God can love or even act in the temporal world (these problems are outlined in my book *The Puzzle of God*. Such issues are, however, outside the scope of this book but they are important, as many philosophers of religion believe that they cast doubt on the coherence of any idea of God as literally timeless. If these philosophers are right, then this would point to a major flaw in the whole Thomist approach. Whether they are or not is still a matter of vexed debate!

Aquinas' approach effectively dissolves the problem of evil, provided his definitions and premises are accepted. By adopting God's perspective rather than that of human beings the problem is largely overcome. From God's perspective, everything is good and God is good since God is fully whatever it is to be God and all desires tend to God.

Aquinas' thought is like a great cathedral, it is magnificent and almost all of it hangs together well. However, acceptance of his approach demands acceptance of certain presuppositions, in particular the view that God is literally timeless and that univocal language cannot be applied to God. It also means looking at the problem of evil from God's perspective rather than that of man. Intellectually, Aquinas' approach has much to commend it, but from a human point of view some may feel that it is lacking. Apart from the problems raised above, it does not address the suffering and pain of this world in a way that takes account of God's fatherhood and of his love for and commitment to his creatures – whether these be human beings or animals. It does not take account of the God who suffers with his creation, nor does it owe anything to what Christ is meant to have revealed of God's nature. It is an intellectual's approach, it is rational and neat but it may have little to say to those for whom suffering and evil is a reality rather than simply an academic question. To maintain the Thomist position in the face of the victims of the holocaust or even of a mother mourning the death of her child from an earthquake may not always be easy.

These shortcomings are serious even if they are not necessarily fatal if one accepts the Thomist perspective. Alternative approaches need, therefore, to be considered.

THREE

The Free Will Defence

Man is the greatest enemy of man. Oppression, injustice, contempt, contumely, violence, sedition, war, calumny, treachery, fraud; by these they mutually torment each other ... The disorders of the mind, though more secret, are not perhaps less dismal or vexatious. Remorse, shame, anguish, rage, disappointment, anxiety, fear, dejection, despair: who has ever passed through life without cruel inroads from these tormentors? How many have scarcely ever felt any better sensations? Labour and poverty, so abhorred by everyone, are the certain lot of the far greater number ...

DAVID HUME, *Dialogues concerning Natural Religion*, Penguin, p.106

The Free Will Defence (FWD) seeks to remove responsibility for evil from God by blaming it on dependent beings who have wilfully misused God's gift of freedom. As such, it is normally directed against moral evil perpetrated by human beings. It cannot be directly used against natural evil unless such evils are blamed on the Devil, and it is accepted that the Devil's fall (from being an angel of God) is also due to an act of angelic free will. We shall discuss this latter possibility which sees the Devil as representing a cosmic source of evil, in due course, but in the meantime we shall concentrate on the straightforward FWD against moral evil.

i) The Free Will Defence outlined

The FWD maintains that God had a reason for allowing evil in the world. The steps in the argument are as follows:

1. Human beings are made for a love relationship with God and this is the highest good of all and the end for which all of us are intended.

2. Love cannot be forced, it must be freely chosen. If, therefore, human beings are to respond in love to God, they must be free to turn towards God or away from God. They must be free to choose between good and evil. Human freedom is a necessary condition for loving God or for loving others.

3. If individuals can choose to be courageous, just, kind, merciful, compassionate, forgiving and gentle, it follows that they must be able to choose to take the opposite path and to be unjust, cruel, vicious, greedy and harsh in their dealings with their fellows. The price for the possibility of the higher virtues is the possibility of the baser vices.

4. Human beings seek happiness and pleasure and try to avoid misery and pain. If some people are to alleviate suffering and to care for others in pain and distress, then pain and distress must be possibilities. The cruel, vicious and malevolent must be able to inflict suffering on others if they are to be truly free, just as the compassionate and kind must be able to help those who suffer.

5. God is omnipotent and he *could* prevent all pain and suffering, but the price of his doing this would be to take away human freedom. It is better to allow human freedom even though this may have terrible consequences than to deprive man of freedom and to turn humans into programmed robots who no longer have

The Free Will Defence

the possibility of discovering what a love relationship with God amounts to.

The FWD rests on the idea that the world is, as John Hick puts it, "a vale of soul making". In a chapter entitled "Soul Making and Suffering" (in *Evil and the God of Love*, Fontana, 1966), Hick argues for the necessity for suffering in order to develop individual souls. Hick rejects the idea that God intended this world as a type of hedonistic paradise. God should not be regarded like a human being building a cage for a pet animal to play in. On this model if the human being was humane he would naturally make his cage as pleasant and healthy as possible. Hick warns of asking the wrong sort of question about the world:

> The question we have to ask is not "Is this the sort of world that an all-powerful and infinitely loving being would create as an environment for his human pets?" . . . The question we have to ask is rather "Is this the kind of world that God might make as an environment in which moral beings may be fashioned, through their own insights and responses, into children of God?"
>
> (cf. Hick's chapter reprinted in Adams & Adams (Eds.)
> *The Problem of Evil*, p.170)

Hick maintains that suffering is a necessary condition for the development of human souls (in this he shares Ireneus' outlook – cf. chapter 1) so that they may come to freely respond to God in love. Hick admits the difficulty of extreme suffering, which does not enable but rather destroys, and at this point retreats behind talk of mystery:

> The mystery of dysteleogical suffering is a real mystery, impenetrable to the rational human mind. It challenges Christian faith with its utterly baffling, alien, destructive meaninglessness. And yet at the same time, detached theological reflection can

note that this very irrationality and this lack of ethical meaning contribute to the world as a place in which true human goodness can occur and in which loving sympathy and compassionate self-sacrifice can take place.

(Adams & Adams (Eds.) p.187)

Keith Ward takes a similar, albeit slightly modified line, saying that God is not primarily interested in human suffering (*Divine Action*, HarperCollins, 1990). Clearly God would deplore and reject such suffering but there is a higher good than pleasure, a good which men and women can dimly glimpse on earth – that is a love relationship between the individual and God which commences in this life and finds its fulfilment and completion after death.

The highest good is human freedom as this is a necessary condition for a relationship with God. God is leading us from human biological life to a spiritual life with him. The existence of suffering and pain is the necessary price that has to be paid for this *as God could order the world in no other way* if this objective were to be achieved.

This is a subtle approach as it defends both God's goodness and his omnipotence. The freedom of human beings is the highest good, and suffering, evil and pain is the necessary price that has to be paid for this freedom. The FWD allows God to be depicted as really loving men and women, and acting in their true, long-term interests in trying to bring them to the highest good of all, a relationship with him. Jesus, as God, can be depicted as fighting against pain, misery and despair and trying to alleviate this. Such pain and misery are *not* what God chooses and Jesus and his followers are committed to minimizing this wherever possible. They are committed to fighting against the forces of injustice and of evil.

One of the crucial issues raised by the FWD is that of what it means to talk of human beings as free.

ii) The nature of freedom

Most people think that they are free, but in practice they recognize that their freedom is greatly constrained. Leibniz suggested two main ways of defining human freedom:

a) Liberty of Spontaneity

It is possible to argue that, although we think we are free to choose between alternatives, this is really because we do not know enough about ourselves. If we really understood the background influences that affect us as well as our own nature, we might see that our actions are totally predictable. As the sciences of genetics and the human mind advance, we may come to see that our room for alternative action is non-existent. We can think of ourselves as free as long as our knowledge of those factors that influence us is not complete – in fact, we are bound by genetic chains as well as the customs and practices of the society in which we were reared and we cannot loose these chains. To take this view is to claim that we have Liberty of Spontaneity.

Anthony Flew defines a free action as an action that is not externally compelled but flows from the nature of the agent. This, he maintains, is how the word "free" is normally used. He takes the example of the sort of person that a man will marry. The man may think that his choice is free, but in fact the choice he makes is greatly constrained by his background. His friends and family will know the sort of person who is likely to appeal to him. He will choose not at random, but freely according to his nature. He is free in that he acts without external constraints. Actions are free not in the sense that they are arbitrary, but simply that they are his choice, arising out of his nature without external compulsion. Flew puts it this way:

> To say that Murdo was free to ask whichever eligible girl of his acquaintance he wanted, and that he chose to ask, was accepted by, and has now married Mairi of his own free will, is not to

say that his actions and choices were uncaused or in principle unpredictable ... Indeed those who knew Murdo may have known what was going to happen long before the date of the wedding ...

(New Essays in Philosophical Theology, p.150)

If this is the case, then just as Murdo's choice was not random but was determined by the person Murdo was, in other words by Murdo's nature, then God could have given all human beings the type of natures which would ensure that they always chose the good. If we were different people, if we had different personalities, we would act differently.

Flew gives another illustration by means of an analogy with post-hypnotic suggestions. A patient can, under hypnosis, be given a series of instructions which he is to carry out after waking – for instance he can be instructed to go to a library at a certain time and borrow a certain book. He may at the same time be told to forget that he had received these instructions. On coming out of the hypnotic trance, he will be obediently unaware of what transpired in it, but will nevertheless at the prescribed time feel a desire to go to the library and borrow the book, a desire that the ordinary resources of the educated intellect will find no difficulty in rationalizing. The person will thus carry out the hypnotic commands whilst seeming both to himself and to others to be doing so of his own free will and for his own reasons. Flew sums up:

> Omnipotence might have, could without contradiction be said to have, created people who would always as a matter of fact choose to do the right thing.

There is no question that the view that man's freedom is wholly determined by his nature is an available philosophic position, but there is something suspect about Flew's example. If the hypnotist told the patient to love her, then the love would certainly not be genuine. Similarly if God manipulated man's nature to bring about the results he sought, then the possibility of real love would be eliminated.

It is difficult to prove that our actions are not, in fact, wholly constrained in the way that this definition of freedom assumes, since it rests on assumptions about future scientific and medical advances which cannot be proved to be false. However, lack of proof does not force us to accept Flew's position which may well be considered to be counterintuitive. Freedom is not just freedom of action as Flew assumes. It is a freedom to choose to make ourselves into different types of being. Hamlet's "to be or not to be" can be seen as expressing this freedom (there are many interpretations of Hamlet and some argue that when he makes this particular speech he is not free as he is not capable of committing suicide). Hamlet can be seen as being aware of the choices that he can make about the sort of person he is to become and he agonizes over these choices. It is the possibility of such agonizing and of making real choices that points towards Liberty of Indifference and against Flew's approach to conditional freedom.

b) Liberty of Indifference

Mackie (*The Miracle of Theism*, p.166) effectively defines Liberty of Indifference as a state in which there is "no set of antecedent sufficient causes for an individual to choose one option as opposed to another". Alternatively it may be defined as the capacity for alternative action which is not wholly determined by our nature. To put it another way, this approach would hold that Hamlet was right to agonize over his choices as they were real choices that had to be made between alternatives and were not determined completely by the type of person Hamlet was.

Kant did not think that it was possible to prove that human beings were free. Certainly it seems a reasonable assumption, even if its status must remain that of an assumption rather than a proven fact. Dostoyevsky in his books continually asserts man's freedom and the possibilities that are open for men and women to surprise, to act against what people consider their nature to be. In *The Brothers Karamazov*, Grushenka, the rather loose moralled but attractive and very human young lady, had been trying to seduce the young novice monk, Alyosha. However, when Alyosha was at his most vulnerable with all his spiritual defences down, it is this same prostitute who "puts him together again". The capacity for human beings to stand out against the programming of the societies in which they live is much greater than many will allow.

If, indeed, we do have Liberty of Indifference, the freedom to act in ways that are not wholly determined by our background and genetic make-up, then perhaps God could not have created us so that we are *both* free *and* never sin. It is to this issue we must now turn.

iii) The Utopia Thesis

Even if human beings do have liberty of indifference, it may still be argued that God could have created them so that they always do what is good. Ninian Smart described this as The Utopia Thesis. He says that a creature not subject to temptation, or to fear, envy, anxiety or guilt would no doubt be innocent but he or she would not be considered morally good. In order to have moral goodness, one must have changeable creatures who can be subject to, and give in to, temptation. Smart says:

> The concept good as applied to humans connects with other concepts such as temptation, courage, generosity, etc. . . . These concepts have no application if men are built wholly good.
>
> (*Omnipotence, Evil and Supermen*, p.188)

If it is, indeed, possible for us to have genuine freedom (Liberty of Indifference) *and at the same time* for God to bring it about that we always act in accordance with the good, then God's failure to bring this state of affairs about is indeed a sure indication that God is not good, at least as we understand the term. This is why the question of what it means for God to be omnipotent is so important. *If God can do things which in our language are logically impossible* (as Descartes maintained) *then God could square the circle, he could bring it about that we are free and yet only do what is right.* His failure to actualize the Utopia Thesis would be a massive indictment of him.

To restate the point – if, as Descartes maintained, God could do the logically impossible, then God *could* have created a world in which both:

1. Men and women were genuinely free, *and*
2. God brought it about that these genuinely free beings never did evil.

If God failed to do this, and if he was capable of it, then God is in an indefensible position. On this basis, God cannot really care for his creation, let alone love individual human beings, at least if the word "love" is used in any sense which remotely resembles what we normally mean by the term. The possibility was open to God to create a world free of pain and suffering and still give individuals the chance to respond to him and he refused to take this. If, therefore, God can do what appears to us to be logically impossible, it seems that we are left with no alternative but to say that, from our point of view, God either does not exist or, if he does, then he is fundamentally evil.

If, however, we adhere to Aquinas' view, then perhaps it simply *is not possible* for God to combine the two positions above. Freedom, if it is genuine, must necessarily leave open the possibility of pain and suffering. Of course, God can set limits to this, but we are then into a different debate (to which we shall return) as to whether the limits that have been set are too wide.

In the last paragraph I said "perhaps it simply is not possible . . ." and the word "perhaps" needs consideration. God had to decide which universe to create. Assume that God could have created a whole range of alternative universes. In one possible world there would be no trees, in another possible world there would be no donkeys, in another possible world almost everyone would inflict pain on each other, in another possible world there would be no good and beauty at all. In many of the possible worlds there are free beings who can choose to act and in the different worlds they act in different ways. If there is an infinite number of such universes, then surely there might have been a universe in which, as a matter of contingent fact, free human beings always freely chose to act rightly and justly?

If there is an infinite range of possible universes that God could have created, it might have been logically possible for God to have brought into existence *that world in which free beings always do what is right*. J. L. Mackie formulates this challenge against the Free Will Defence as follows:

> If there is no logical possibility in a man freely choosing the good on one, or on several occasions, there cannot be a logical possibility in his freely choosing the good on every occasion. God was not, then, faced with a choice between making innocent automata and making beings who in acting freely, would sometimes go wrong: there was open to him the obviously better possibility of making beings who would act freely but would always do right. Clearly his failure to avail himself of this possibility is inconsistent with his being omnipotent and wholly good.
>
> (*Evil and Omnipotence*, p.209)

If, Mackie argues, it is logically possible that one being should always do what is right (and Christians maintain that this happened in the case of Jesus), then is it not also logically possible that a world could exist in which everyone did what was right? Given that there were an infinite number of possible worlds that God could have created, God had the possibility of bringing into existence the best of all possibilities, namely that world in which humans had genuine freedom and yet they always did what was right. God's failure to take this option proves, it might be held, that God is not good.

Alvin Plantinga has argued in support of the Free Will Defence and his approach could be applied against Mackie as well. Plantinga rejects the idea of an infinite number of possible worlds. His argument runs as follows. Assume there is a corrupt figure called Curly Smith who is mayor of Boston. It is part of Curly's very nature to be corrupt (this is a Lutheran idea and denies the basic goodness of human beings). Plantinga puts it like this:

> . . . it was not within God's power to actualize a world in which Curly produces moral good but no moral evil. Every world God could have actualized is such that if Curly is significantly free in it, he takes at least one wrong action . . .
> . . . perhaps God knows in advance that no matter what circumstances he places Curly in, so long as he leaves him sufficiently free, he will take at least one wrong action.
>
> ("God, Evil and the metaphysics of freedom" in *The Problem of Evil*, Ed. Adams & Adams, OUP, 1990, p.102)

Discussion of possible worlds has had a long history in philosophy, starting probably with Leibniz, as a way of setting out possibly conceivable states of affairs. Plantinga claims that in every possible world in which Curly could exist he would necessarily be corrupt. There could not be a world in which Curly was not corrupt, because then he would not be Curly. Curly suffers, Plantinga maintains, from "transworld depravity" – in other words he is depraved in every possible world in which he could exist. Plantinga continues:

> What is important about the idea of transworld depravity is that if a person suffers from it, then it was not within God's power to actualize any world in which that person is significantly free

but does no wrong . . . But clearly it is possible that everyone suffers from transworld depravity . . .

(pp.102–3)

If we follow Plantinga's suggestion and assume that every human being suffers from transworld depravity, then it follows that God could not have created human beings without them being depraved since depravity is a part of the very nature of human beings, it is part of their essential essence:

If every creaturely essence suffers from transworld depravity, then it was beyond the power of God himself to create a world containing moral good but no moral evil . . . Under these conditions, God could have created a world containing no moral evil only by creating one without significantly free persons.

(p.105)

The question is, of course, why depravity *has* to be part of the essence of human nature. This does not seem obvious. If God can do everything that is logically possible, there seems no reason why human beings must *necessarily* have a depraved nature. This is a matter of contingent fact, not a necessary truth. Mackie's challenge could still stand because God had the power to create beings who did not sin even if we had to coin another name for them.

iv) The FWD defended

There are two sustainable answers to Mackie's challenge but they depend on two different conceptions of God. *If*:

1. God is timeless then it does not make sense to talk of God choosing between alternatives. Aquinas holds (ST 1a, 25, 6) that God could create different worlds but at this point there is a flaw in his logic.

If God is literally timeless and has no potential to be other than he is (as Aquinas affirms), then it follows that God has no potential to act other than as he does act. God does not deliberate between alternatives and, therefore, the idea of God "deciding" is out of place. Timeless God creates that which his unchangeable nature brings him to create. There is only one possible universe, the one we have. This universe, because it is created by timeless God who is defined as perfectly good (meaning metaphysically complete and unchanging) must, because of this definition, be the perfectly good universe. Therefore the very idea of a range of possible universes from which God could choose is flawed. If God is timeless, then God's true freedom means a freedom to act wholly in accordance with God's nature without external constraint. This freedom God has, but it does not permit a freedom to deliberate and choose between alternatives (it is interesting to note that on this view God's freedom is the same as the view of human freedom proposed by Flew above – in other words freedom entirely determined by nature).

Plantinga is not working with a timeless model of God, as the idea of such a God choosing between different possible universes is not viable. Given the immutable and unchangeable nature of timeless God and the fact that this God has no potential to be other than he is, timeless God has no potential to choose (at least as the term is normally used) between alternative courses of action.

2. The second alternative is to see God not as timeless but as an everlasting spirit. In this case it would make sense for God to choose between alternative universes.

Even if a wide range of universes were a possibility, however, the everlasting God could not know which universe would be the one in which no-one sinned, since the everlasting God would not know what future free actions human beings would perform. The everlasting God knows the past and the present perfectly, but the future is "open", it is undecided to the extent that humans can make free choices.

If Jocelyn is genuinely free to marry Simon, then the everlasting God cannot know in advance whether or not she will do so. God may know that Simon is the sort of sensitive, kind, intelligent and understanding person whom Jocelyn would be likely to want to marry, but as God is in time, God cannot *know* that she will do so.

It follows, therefore, that the everlasting God's lack of knowledge of the future free actions of human beings limits this God's ability to choose between alternative universes. God made human beings who were free, God made the best possible universe, but what human beings did with their freedom was not predictable. God had to take the risk of giving people freedom, knowing that abuse of this freedom was a real possibility.

This latter picture of God as an everlasting spirit, and man with genuine freedom, can be illustrated by reference to Eve. God could have created the world with contingent beings who had the freedom to do or to refrain from doing evil actions. This was the situation portrayed at the beginning of the Book of Genesis. God gave Eve the choice. It was a logical possibility that Eve would not sin, but God gave her the freedom to choose and God *did not know what she would do*. Eve abused this freedom and had to take the consequences – she is shown as being cast out of the garden. What is more, her choices, and ours, affect future generations. The story of Genesis can, therefore, be held to illustrate an important truth – that in giving human beings freedom, God chose to limit himself and not to control their actions.

God has, as Hick puts it (in *Evil and the God of Love*) embarked, through the use of evolution, on "the hazardous adventure of individual freedom" and God did not know how humans would use the freedom they were given. This seems closer to the straightforward biblical views. For instance Genesis 6:5 says:

> The Lord saw that the wickedness of man was great upon the earth, and that every imagination of his heart was only evil

continually. And the Lord was sorry that he had made man on the earth, and it grieved him to his heart.

The question is whether we should take biblical language such as this as expressing a literal truth about God or whether it should rather be seen as a metaphor. If:

a) the passage is taken literally, then God is in time. God created the world but did not know the outcome. God is surprised and disappointed by the actions of men and responds to these actions. Man's sin, as a result of the gift of free will, is seen as a cause of grief to God. God sends prophets in response to man's failure to live up to God's requirements and finally, God, out of love, has to send his only Son to suffer and to die as the only way of bringing humanity back to a love relationship with him. God, therefore, responds and reacts to human actions. If, on the other hand –

b) the passage is treated as a metaphor, then God can be seen as timeless. God cannot grieve as we grieve since this requires time, and human emotion cannot be applied to God. God had no choice (at least not as we understand choice, in terms of deliberating between alternatives) as to which universe to create and we call this universe good because it is created by the metaphysically good or perfect God.

Everything, therefore, hangs on which view of God is taken. Both answers are satisfactory philosophically. The latter approach will entail our taking an approach to the problem of evil similar to that discussed in chapter 2, and the whole idea of God's choosing between different possible worlds, which Mackie suggests, is not therefore possible. The alternative is the former view, which will entail an everlasting God, a suffering God but a God who cannot *know* the future free actions of human beings and has to respond to these actions. In this case God could not choose between different universes so as to bring about the universe in which free individuals will always do what is right, as God did not know what human beings would do with their freedom. On neither view, therefore, does Mackie's charge succeed.

At this point the critics could return to the attack. They could claim that, even if we have to have Liberty of Indifference, there are *some* constraints on our freedom due to our nature as human beings. God could have made man so that, out of our own God-given moral resources, we would always overcome temptation and act correctly or, at the least, that we would overcome temptation more often than we do. Pain may have a value in certain circumstances – when it is bravely borne it can ennoble the character. However, a great deal of physical suffering is not ennobling. It is, indeed, probably the irrationality of much of the suffering in the world which causes moral revulsion against both natural disasters and the base turpitude of many men and women. To argue that many people starve so that others may have the opportunity to be generous to them seems highly unconvincing.

If the soul-making position is to be maintained, it is necessary to show that an omnipotent God who can do anything within the realms of logic and his own nature (as the limits of logic are the limits of what makes sense – square circles are simply nonsense) *could not* have made the world better than it is and still have obtained the same results. This is not an easy position for which to argue. We also need to recognize the sort of value judgement that we are making and with which critics may mock the believer's own claims. Thus Flew quotes Cardinal Newman (in *On Anglican Difficulties*, VIII):

> The Catholic Church "holds that it were better for the sun and moon to drop from heaven, for the earth to fail, and for all the many millions who are upon it to die . . . in extremest agony . . . than that one soul, I will not say should be lost, but should

commit one single venial sin, should tell one wilful untruth . . . or steal one poor farthing without excuse."

Many would hold that the idea that many should die in extremest agony rather than one person should commit a single minor sin verges on the obscene, and this charge will have to be taken seriously. We need to recognize that the FWD rests on the view that the pain and suffering in the world are a worthwhile price to pay for the development of the higher spiritual values. As we shall see, this is a position that can and should be challenged.

Before considering this challenge (in chapter 5) however, we must turn to the problem of natural evil.

Summary

The Free Will Defence maintains that it is necessary that God should allow evil and suffering to take place if human beings are to be free to enter into a genuine two-way love relationship with him. God could not have ordered the world in any other way if the possibility of this love relationship was to be open. Supporters of the FWD need to show that the world could not have been ordered in a way which would have involved less suffering and evil if the same result was to be achieved, and they also need to maintain that the freedom is worth the price. Both these assumptions can be challenged.

FOUR

Natural Evil

God's power, we allow, is infinite. Whatever he wills is
executed. But neither man nor any other animal is happy:
Therefore he does not will their happiness . . . Look around
this universe. What an immense profusion of beings,
animated and organized, sensible and active! You admire
the prodigious variety and fecundity. But inspect a little
more closely these living existences . . . How hostile and
destructive to each other! How insufficient all of them for
their own happiness! How contemptible or odious to the
spectator! The whole presents nothing but the idea of a
blind nature, impregnated by a great and vivifying principle,
and pouring from her lap, without discernment or parental
care, her maimed and aborted children!

DAVID HUME, *Dialogues concerning*
Natural Religion, Penguin, pp.108 & 121

Moral evils are those evils which are under man's control and which
can, therefore, be attributed to the free acts of human agents. Many
of the ills of the world, however, cannot be explained in this way.
They include, for instance:

1. The distress caused to animals over hundreds of thousands of years.
2. The suffering and torment inflicted on human beings by natural
   disasters such as earthquakes, tidal waves, volcanoes, storms,
   tempests and the like.
3. The pain resulting from disorders to the human body such as
   smallpox, cholera, tuberculosis, diphtheria and cancer.
4. The way in which the human body is made so that, for instance,

childbirth causes great pain and diseases such as arthritis and backache cause continuous distress – due apparently, if there is a God who designed human bodies, to poor design.

5. Psychological illnesses which are due to inherited defects.

Even if the Free Will Defence against the problem of moral evil succeeded, the existence of natural evil may be held to rule out the possibility of belief in an all-powerful and benevolent God.

We have already considered one answer to this problem. If God is literally timeless and had no potential, then God is pure actuality and this world is actualized as a result of God's nature. God freely ("free" here meaning God's ability to act according to his nature without external constraint) brings this world into existence. Just as God is perfectly good – God is metaphysically complete and perfect – so similarly this world is perfectly good. It is metaphysically perfect and manifests God's glory in the whole hierarchy of creation. Aquinas and Augustine before him showed no consideration, for instance, of animal suffering. Augustine seems to see little difference between animal suffering brought about by old age and one animal tearing another to bits. He seems to consider that animal suffering is arranged for human welfare or to show the glory of God and does not see it as an evil at all.

Many, however, are not content with this solution. They want to say that this is not the best of all possible worlds that God could have created. Either natural evils *are* evils, they are not part of an ideal world and, possibly, represent a disorder in creation or, on the other hand, God had no alternative but to create a world which included these evils. Holders of these views reject the idea that earthquakes, tidal waves, extreme animal suffering and the like are not evils. They *either*:

a) Want to remove responsibility for natural evils from God by blaming these evils on, for instance, the action of fallen beings such as devils or else to blame these problems on man's own actions, *or*

b) To show for what good reason God would have allowed these evils to take place.

We must now turn to consider three of the main methods that have been used to explain the existence of natural evil.

i) The Devil and natural evil

The Devil is held to be the chief of the fallen angels although there is no single consistent view of the Devil in the Old and New Testaments. The serpent, in the story of Adam and Eve, has traditionally been held to be the embodiment of the Devil and it was through the Devil that "death entered the world" (Wisdom 2:24). In the Book of Job, the Devil is clearly portrayed as a tempter and tormentor of man, although still subservient to God – he has to obtain God's permission for what he intends to do to poor Job. In Zechariah's vision (Zechariah 3:1–2), the Devil acts as the accuser of the High Priest, Joshua.

The Devil is much more prominent in the New Testament than in the Old. He tempts Jesus in the wilderness and throughout the gospels he shows his opposition to Jesus through the demon spirits. He is recognized as the prince of this world, but Jesus is held to have broken his power. At the Last Judgement, the Devil and all his followers will depart into everlasting punishment.

St Augustine held that the Devil's fall was due to pride, he refused to obey God and his disruptive effects in the world were a consequence of this first sin. The Devil's initial sin was held to have fixed him in evil and there seemed to be no room for him to reform.

The Devil tempted Adam, and Adam's failure to resist temptation was not only evil in itself but also had evil consequences that spoilt every aspect of future human life. All aspects of man's life from the labour of hard work and the inability of reason to guide the actions of men were affected by Adam's failure. One problem with this account is that the idea of man falling from a state of perfection may not stand up to scientific enquiry – history simply was not like that. The long evolutionary process has seen man fighting his way up from a much more primitive form of existence – not falling from a higher sphere to a lower. However, the lack of historicity in respect of Adam and Eve does *not* rule out the existence of the Devil and the possibility of blaming him for the natural evil in the world. It is, perhaps, interesting that Jesus seems to resist blaming past errors for present ills. Thus he says in John 9:3 –

> It is not that this man sinned nor his parents, but that the glory of God might be manifested in him.

There are two primary approaches to the problems of the Devil's sin:

1. Aquinas, and later the Dominicans who followed his ideas, held that the Devil, being a fallen angel, knew that he could not obtain equality with God, but he and the other demons wished to obtain eternal happiness or beatitude by the exercise of their own powers rather than by submission to God. The Devil made one decision and became fixed in evil as a result of this.

2. The Franciscans, by contrast, followed Duns Scotus and maintained that the Devil committed many different types of sin before becoming obstinately or habitually evil. Lucifer, they mainted, desired equality with God and his chief sin consisted in the immoderate love of his own excellence.

Both views are still held. It is surprising that, given the importance the New Testament and the whole Christian tradition up to the late Middle Ages placed on the Devil, very little attention is today paid to him and the possibility of the Devil's existence has become almost a matter of laughter. Professor Stewart Sutherland in *God, Jesus and Belief* (Blackwell, 1984) argues that just as theologians have largely abandoned belief in the Devil, so they can also abandon belief in God as a father who is independent of the world he created. Sutherland goes on to develop a revisionary view of Christianity which requires neither God nor the Devil to make sense of central Christian insights into the human condition.

Alvin Plantinga, a theologian working from within the Reformed tradition, is one figure who has taken the Devil seriously in a modern discussion of the problem of evil. He claims that it is possible to attribute natural evil to the Devil's free decision to fall from grace. He puts it like this:

> St Augustine believes that natural evil (except for what can be attributed to God's punishment) is in fact to be ascribed to the activity of beings that are free and rational but non-human. The Free Will defender need not assert that this is *true*; he says only that it is possible . . . It is possible that all natural evil is due to the free activity of non-human persons, and there is no world God could have created which contains a more favourable balance of good over evil with respect to the free activity of the non-human persons it contains.
>
> ("God, Evil and the metaphysics of freedom" in
> *The Problem of Evil*, Ed. Adams & Adams, OUP, 1990, p.108)

God gave the angels free will and it is possible that the Devil chose to exercise this and to turn away from God – he then wrought havoc in the world and disrupted God's perfect creation. God could not intervene to prevent this without taking away not only human but also angelic freedom. Plantinga is, in effect, using the Free Will Defence, which is usually applied to moral evil, to attempt to resolve the problem of natural evil. It is important to emphasize that Plantinga does not claim that the Devil does, in fact, exist, only that the existence of the Devil who is responsible for natural evil is a possibility. This, he considers, is all that the supporter of the Free Will Defence has to show. The Free Will Defence is being used here to explain natural evil and this is what makes Plantinga's approach distinctive among many philosophers of religion – normally this defence is only applied to the problem of moral evil.

Anthony Flew has rejected this approach: he says the existence of the Devil has not been proved. However, this is not a good argument. The problem of evil itself arises from the claimed existence of a creator God who loves his creation and it is debatable whether this can be proved. The Devil may, indeed, be a hypothesis, but it is a hypothesis with a long history and empirical grounds alone cannot be allowed to rule the hypothesis out of order. The possible existence and role of the Devil or evil forces is something to which I will return in some detail in the second part of this book.

Other questions can, however, be raised to challenge Plantinga's account. In particular, it is hard to see what functions angels necessarily play in creation. If the purpose of creation is to provide an arena in which free individuals can be brought into a personal relationship with God, why is there any need for angels at all, particularly in view of the enormous disruption that the fall of one of these angels, on Plantinga's account, is meant to have caused?

One answer to this might be to borrow from the Thomist approach and to say that the universe is a manifestation of God's glory and, to manifest this adequately, a complete hierarchy of creation is necessary. Angels are part of this hierarchy. This approach, whilst valid, does not place man at the pinnacle of creation – although it may, of course, be argued that it is mere human conceit to want to do this. With the rise of "Green" environmental concern, Aquinas' position can be seen as more persuasive as man begins to recognize that he is part of a wider creation.

Possibly the chief weakness of trying to blame the Devil for the existence of natural evil is that many religious believers no longer believe in such a force of evil. In addition, the overwhelming evidence of fossil records and evolutionary studies seems to point to the emergence of the solar system and animal, plant and human life over hundreds of millions of years by a gradual process operating according to constant laws of nature. There is no evidence at all for some paradise-like state free from all evil which was then corrupted by an evil intelligence. Natural laws operate with apparently uniform regularity and the real question raised by natural evils is why the laws of the universe are as they are.

ii) Is this the best of all possible worlds?

If God is literally timeless, I have argued that the question as to whether this is the best possible world does not arise, as God could not have created any alternative world. If there are not a number of possible worlds, there can be no best possible world. This is the most perfect world – just as God is perfectly God. God is perfect in that God is fully whatever it is to be God, without us thereby knowing what it means for God to be God. Similarly it can be held that the created universe is fully whatever it is to be the created universe. This necessarily follows from the Thomist system and argument is not really possible – although there is no reason why critics should accept Aquinas' use of terms.

We do not, however, have to go along with the assumption that God is timeless and that God's choice of universe is determined by his nature. Instead, God may be held to be *everlasting*. He may be without beginning and without end, but unchanging in his love and care for his creation. If this view is taken, then a very different picture emerges.

Leibniz argued that since God is both good and omnipotent, he will have an overriding reason to create the best of all possible worlds. This must, therefore, be the best of all possible worlds, since an all-good and omnipotent God would create no other. As he says:

> This supreme wisdom, united to a goodness that is no less infinite, cannot but have chosen the best . . . If there were not the best among all possible worlds, God would not have produced any

. . . There is an infinitude of possible worlds amongst which God must needs have chosen the best.

Richard Swinburne rejects this approach as he does not think there can be, conceptually, any one "best possible world" (*The Existence of God*, p.113). Even if there was such a world, Swinburne follows Aquinas in saying God would be under no obligation to create it. A finite world must have a finite number of beings. Surely, Swinburne argues, one more or less such being would not necessarily make the world better or worse. If this is the case, then it no longer makes sense to say that God would have an overriding reason to create a single "best possible world".

Swinburne cautions against two false conclusions from the above:

1. Leibniz says that if there were no best possible world, God would have no reason to create any world. This is wrong. Swinburne says that God may have had reason to create *some* world and *not* to create other worlds. This, however, does not mean that there is any single world that God has reason to create. A man has reason to buy a certain sort of house – perhaps one that is structurally sound, comfortable to live in, well designed, economical to run, etc., but this does not mean that he has reason to buy *one particular* house.

So God may have had reason to create a universe with trees, but this does not mean that he has reason to create a universe with the precise number of leaves on the trees that there are in the world at the present time.

2. It is wrong to say that God might have created *any* world. There will be worlds that God would have good reason *not* to create. God's choice lies between those worlds which he would have no overriding reason not to create.

Even if, Swinburne continues, there were a single best possible world, God would have no moral obligation to create this world since God cannot have a moral obligation to nonexistent beings (Aquinas made a similar point which we discussed on p.29). There might have been another world in which Peter Vardy was crippled. If this is so, then surely in creating me God does not wrong my Doppelganger? If we can have no moral obligation to nonexistents, then similarly God can have no moral responsibility prior to the Creation. The idea of God having any moral obligation to his creation then falls away.

So what sort of world might God have reason to create? Swinburne analyses four possibilities:

a) **World Group One**
This would consist of that group of worlds which contained an unchanging set of immortal, humanly free agents. The world and its people would have their imperfections, but the world would be *perfectible* by the co-operation of the people within it within a finite time. In other words, within a limited time, the world could be brought into a happy and beautiful state. Once this point was reached, there would be nothing further to do.

b) **World Group Two**
This consists of that group of worlds which contain an unchanging set of immortal, humanly free agents *but* there is an infinite number of such agents *and* there are no limits to the improvements that could be made – i.e. the world is infinitely improvable.

So: There are an infinite number of free agents; an infinite degree of improvability and infinite time. However, there is no birth in this world and Swinburne considers this to be a lack.

c) **World Group Three**
Again, there are immortal agents, but the number of these can be increased through birth. This number can be extended infinitely.

d) **World Group Four**
Here there is death as well as birth. There is a limitless ability to

improve the world. Each generation can advance or retard the world – but only to a small extent.

Swinburne considers the fourth group of worlds to be the most attractive. A world with birth and death and where there is limitless ability to improve the world is the ideal. But why is death so important and attractive? What makes death necessary to the best possible series of worlds? Swinburne suggests five reasons:

i) If agents could not die, there would be a certain degree of harm that agents could not inflict on each other. Everyone would be immortal. In this vital respect, human agents would not share the creative power of God *unless* there were death. Without death, God would not be trusting the creatures he created.

ii) A world without death would be a world in which ultimate self-sacrifice could not take place. *The ultimate sacrifice is the sacrifice of oneself* and without death this would not be possible. Cheerfulness and patience in the face of absolute disaster would be ruled out.

iii) A limited life span concentrates the attention on the way a human being spends his time. If the human life span were infinite, this would not happen.

iv) A world with birth but no death would be a world in which the young never had a free hand, as the older generation would always dominate.

v) It would be wrong for God to give man limitless power to hurt others. Death, therefore, limits the amount of suffering that one person can inflict on another.

Swinburne concludes that God would have reason to create a world falling under World Group Four. This particular world belongs to the fourth world group. *So this world is of a type that God would have had a reason to create.*

Why God should have created this particular world out of all the other possible worlds under World Group Four is a question that, Swinburne considers, cannot be answered.

Of course, there is a challenge that can be made here. Why should God not have created a world belonging to World Group Four but where there is less suffering than is found in this world? Swinburne has an answer to this. He maintains that the demand for lesser suffering is a demand for a *toy world* – a world where nothing matters very much; where individuals cannot inflict real harm on each other; where human free actions do not have significant consequences.

Further Swinburne says that out of love for man, God provides two ways of limiting suffering:

i) The human body is so constructed that, when pain passes a certain point, the individual passes out, and

ii) Death sets a temporal limit on the amount of any suffering. However much pain we endure, we will die after seventy or eighty years and our pain is therefore limited.

The presence of natural evil is not taken into account on the above model, and Swinburne deals with this in a slightly different way. He maintains that this is a do–it–yourself kit world, a world in which God has arranged the conditions for man to bring about changes and to advance the development of the world. The world must be as it is for three reasons:

I. The argument from the need for knowledge

The world needs to be law-abiding so that human agents learn the consequences of their actions. It is the existence of natural law that points most clearly to God. God is a "simpler" explanation of the existence of natural laws than if these laws were assumed to be a brute fact. The universe is an interlocking whole which is completely law-abiding, enabling consequences to be predicted.

Natural disasters teach human beings to take precautions for their own benefit and in order to improve their world. If human agents are to have knowledge of evil, evil must occur and these agents must learn from the consequences. Human beings must learn by experience.

Swinburne rejects a world in which human beings are given the requisite knowledge directly. If such knowledge were given directly, God would not be ambiguous enough – his presence would be too obvious.

2. Argument for higher order goods

This argument maintains that various evils are necessary for higher order goods. Thus suffering is necessary for there to be suffering to bear cheerfully; there must be fear in order to have courage; there must be vice for there to be virtue. The existence of natural evil thus gives human beings the opportunity to be at their best.

3. Man should have access to a full range of possible experiences

A world in which we did not know of suffering and of pain, of the desolation of orphans and of the rejection of lovers would be a less good world than this one. Thus the Psalmist sings:

It is good for me that I have been in trouble

(Ps. 119:71)

Swinburne admits that if the whole of a human life consisted of such trouble and distress, then this would be an argument against his approach, but he maintains that this is rarely the case. In the vast majority of cases, troubles, hardships and sufferings are mixed with a variety of joys and goods.

Swinburne, therefore, rejects the idea of any *single* best possible world, but maintains that this world is the sort of world which a good God would have reason to create. Why this world, specifically, was created rather than another world belonging to the same group is a question that cannot be answered. Only if God had created a world which belonged to a less good world group would the problem of evil be a real problem. John Hick, in similar vein, argues that God would not have reason to create a world in which there was pointless, futile human suffering. The problem comes in deciding whether suffering *is* pointless and futile. Certainly much human suffering seems to fall into this category – whether it is correct to so place it will largely depend on individual preconceptions.

Of course, many would disagree with Swinburne's premises. They might maintain that the limits of pain and suffering have been set too wide – there is simply too much distress that can be inflicted by natural evils and also by human beings. They might argue that it is a very odd sort of God which will allow, for instance:

a) young children to die in great agony from cancers while the parents watch helplessly. A world without some types of diseases (not necessarily eliminating all diseases or all pain) would have been possible and would still have allowed the higher virtues of courage, bravery and fortitude.

b) earthquakes which kill hundreds of thousands of people. The world could well have been designed so that the underlying geological structure did not operate in the way it does. God can do anything that is logically possible and it seems perfectly within the bounds of logical possibility for a world to have been designed so that the earth's geology had a greater degree of stability. Such a world would still be law-abiding, but the laws would be such that major natural disaster which were not preventable were not so common.

c) the torture systematically inflicted on one group of people by another – for instance in Stalin's death camps; in the Nazi concentration camps or the psychological and physical torture inflicted by secret police forces in various countries who pass electric current through human genitals; use drugs to bring people to the absolute limits of human agony without allowing them the (supposedly God-given) privilege of passing out from the pain. The demand for narrower limits, it may be held, is not a demand for a "toy world" as Swinburne suggests, but for rather narrower limits to the possible suffering that the human body can tolerate.

In addition, two further points need to be made:

d) If every event in the universe (except, possibly, humanly free actions) is held to be due to the will of God, then it follows that God not only allows earthquakes and volcanoes but actually brings them about. Swinburne's model, by contrast, of a natural order that forms a "do-it-yourself kit world" makes God into an absent creator rather than a God who is immanent in every aspect of creation.

e) Christian theology has held that heaven is meant to be a place where there is a perfect heavenly society under the rule of God, yet there is no death in heaven. Swinburne's claim, therefore, that death is necessary, seems suspect. There may even be free will in heaven – depending on how seriously the idea of the fall of the Devil is taken. Satan was an angel who, although he beheld the face of God, chose to rebel and to abandon allegiance to God. He was free to do this – with disastrous consequences for the world. Jesus certainly seems to recognize this. The New Testament, in the story of the temptation in the wilderness, indicates that the Devil had power over the earth and the earth was, in a real sense, "in the Devil's gift".

If the Devil could freely choose to fall, having dwelt in the presence of God and if heaven is the place to which "the saved" are destined if they make the right choices in this life, then why, it may be argued, is not the world as we know it rather more similar to heaven? In heaven there is no death, there is no suffering but still there is a freedom to rebel against God and to disrupt God's plan for creation – why cannot earth be more like heaven?

Swinburne's approach, therefore, like that of Aquinas, can be challenged because of the number of assumptions that he has to make which, on examination, prove to be somewhat debatable. There seems no good reason why we should accept that this world could not be improved and that the amount of suffering due to natural evil should not be reduced.

iii) Matter as evil

Plato (in *Timaeus*) considered that the Demiurge fashioned the universe out of pre-existent matter using the perfect Forms as a model. However, the universe was in time whilst the Forms were timeless and spaceless and the matter itself, which the Demiurge did not create, imposed limits on his creative ability. The Demiurge did as well as he was able – given the matter with which he had to work.

This has been an attractive and influential picture. If we use metaphors like the potter and the clay, then this is quite compatible with the Christian God fashioning pre-existent matter to form the universe. Justin Martyr was one of a number of early Church Fathers who took over Plato's idea and said that the Christian God did not create out of nothing (*ex nihilo*), but used matter that had always existed. This approach was also taken by the Gnostics and is based on a cosmic dualism – the view that there are, ultimately, two separate and irreducible substances, God and matter. It did not, however, find favour with the Church since it maintained that matter was independent of God. Ireneus, in particular, rejected this view and held that God created matter from nothing. If this were not the case, then there would be something apart from God, something that did not owe its existence to God. God would, indeed, be limited by the structure of this matter.

It seems, therefore, that although the existence of matter independent of God could indeed be used to solve the problem of evil, the price for taking this route is a very high one as it would force theologians to accept a much more limited view of God. God would no longer be totally sovereign – his omnipotence would be much curtailed. He would simply be unable to do anything about the existence of evil in the world since this was due to the recalcitrant nature of the material with which he had to operate. God, poor fellow, was doing the best he could and could not be blamed for his failure to achieve perfection. Full marks, we might say, for effort – pity that the potter did not have better clay with which to work.

Grace Jantzen (*God's World, God's Body*, DLT, 1983) develops an interesting alternative idea to the above. She rejects a cosmic dualism and instead argues that the universe is God's body. God is not, therefore, apart from the universe – God is literally embodied in the universe. Just as I am more than my flesh, bones and internal organs, so God transcends the physical universe – not in the sense of being apart from it, but God is "more" than the component parts of the material cosmos. On this view, both good and evil are a part of God. A theodicy is still, she admits, necessary to explain the existence of evil, but at least evil is not seen as a force independent of God. Because of this there is some hope that it may be overcome.

Jantzen's approach, while innovative and interesting, does not, however, help us to resolve the problem of evil. If matter were independent of God, then a solution to the problem of evil could, indeed, be found – even though the price is very high in terms of the restrictions this will place on God. If matter is God's body, then the problem of evil returns with all its force. The problem is no greater on this view than on the traditional view of a God who creates *ex nihilo*, but the problem still exists.

Summary

The Free Will Defence may be held to explain suffering which can be attributed to the actions of human beings, but the existence of natural evil remains a problem for the theist. The Devil can be imported as a hypothesis to explain this evil, but it is difficult to see why an omnipotent and wholly good God should need to have given free will to angels who then fell from grace and wrought havoc in the world if his real concern was to bring human beings to a relationship with him, or why this God could not have prevented the resulting evil.

Natural evil can be explained by attributing it to the orderly workings of the universe. The advantages of natural laws operating regularly so that human beings have the ability to learn about them, can be held to outweigh the suffering that is caused. This, however, raises questions as to whether such evil was really necessary and whether the sufferings caused to human beings and animals over millions of years is really worth the price.

Lastly, if God did not create the universe from nothing and instead worked with pre-existent matter, then natural evil may be due to the inherent nature of this matter. God is then exonerated from blame, but at the price of his omnipotence being curtailed.

None of these solutions seems particularly convincing philosophically. Whilst the Free Will Defence may be persuasive, the presence of natural evil seems to represent a more powerful attack on the credibility of belief in an omnipotent and wholly good creator.

FIVE

Is It All Worth It?

> Have not all pious divines and preachers (said that) this life
> is but a moment in comparison with eternity. The present
> evil phenomena, therefore, are rectified in other regions,
> and in some future period of existence . . . And the eyes
> of men, being then open to a wider view of things . . . trace,
> with adoration, the benevolence and rectitude of the deity.
>
> DAVID HUME, *Dialogues concerning*
> *Natural Religion*, Penguin, p.110

Nelson Pike argued that belief in God is logically inconsistent since:

A being who is omnipotent and omniscient would have no
morally sufficient reason for allowing instances of evil.

("Hume on Evil" *Philosophical Review*, 1963, pp.180–97)

Roderick Chisholm in an article "Divine Goodness and the Problem
of Evil" (Religious Studies 1966–7 pp.95–107 reprinted in Adams &
Adams (Eds.) *The Problem of Evil*, OUP 1990) replies to Pike's
challenge. He claims that any believer in God must be committed
to holding that any evil that exists is defeated by a greater good.
Chisholm sums up his position as follows:

Epicurus says that if God is able but unwilling to prevent evil
then he is malevolent. But if the evil in the world is defeated
and contained in a larger whole that is absolutely good, one should
rather say that, if God had been able but unwilling to create such
evil then he would be malevolent. The theodicist must appeal

to the concept of *defeat* – that he can deal with the problem of evil *only* by saying that the evils in the world are defeated . . . What possible state of affairs could thus serve to defeat the evil that is in the world? The wise theodicist should, I think, say that he does not know . . .

(Adams & Adams, p.68)

Chisholm in claiming that the believer in a good, omnipotent God must claim that the undoubted existence of evil is defeated or made worthwhile by the existence of some higher good seen as part of a wider whole, even though he or she may not know what this good or wider whole is. This is, however, an inadequate intellectual answer as Ivan Karamazov makes clear.

Dostoyevsky's novel *The Brothers Karamazov* (Book 5, chapter 4, Penguin) contains, in my view, the most effective attack against God ever produced. The novel is the story of three brothers, Ivan, Dimitri and Alyosha. Alyosha is a novice monk, living in a monastery close to the Karamazov home and much influenced by a good and holy elder monk named Zossima. Ivan, his worldly-wise brother, returns from the big city after an absence of a number of years and the two brothers get acquainted. The novel contains a long dialogue between the two of them.

Ivan is an atheist, yet he believes in God. This, in itself, is odd as normally an atheist is someone who does not believe in God. Ivan's atheism is, however, of a particular and virulent type (it is discussed clearly and well in Stewart Sutherland's book *Atheism and the Rejection of God*, Blackwell, 1983). He believes that God exists, yet he rejects God's creation and is in rebellion against God. He thus rejects Alyosha's holiness and obedience to the will of God.

Ivan's attack on and rejection of God is so subtle and convincing because he starts from a position with which almost everyone would identify, the suffering of innocent children. By means of a series of horrific examples (which we know that Dostoyevsky took from Russian newspapers of the time and which actually happened), Ivan asks Alyosha to consider the problem of evil. He does not consider the suffering of adults – they have "eaten the apple"; perhaps they themselves might be blamed for the evil that occurs. Instead he concentrates on the extreme suffering of those whom traditional Christianity has considered to be innocent, children under the age of seven. He gives three examples which can be paraphrased as follows:

1. A young girl wets her bed at night. Her mother covers her in her own excrement and locks her, naked, in the outside privy all night. Ivan asks Alyosha whether anything can possibly justify the tears of this little girl as she bangs with her tiny fists on the door of the privy and weeps tears of despair to her "dear kind God".

Can any eventual state of happiness either on earth or in heaven possibly justify the suffering of this little girl?

2. A young boy throws a stone and injures the leg of one of the favourite hunting dogs belonging to the local Lord. At the next hunt, the Lord notices the animal limping and asks who did the damage. He orders the young boy and his parents to be brought before him. He then has the boy stripped and sets him off running across the fields. His pack of hounds are then set on the boy whom they chase and tear to pieces in front of his watching parents.

Ivan says to Alyosha that he knows that at the final judgement the young boy, his parents and the Lord may all be united and may all join hands in shouting . "Hosannah", but he will not accept this. He wants revenge. Again he is making the point that the sufferings of the boy and his parents cannot possibly be justified by any eventual state of bliss and concord.

3. The Turks, Ivan says, are held to love children. When Turkish soldiers were at war in Southern Russia, they used to make babies

smile by playing with the babies, waving their gun barrels in front of their faces. The babies reached up their little hands to grasp the barrels and laughed – whereupon the Turks pulled the trigger and blew the babies' brains out. They also took pleasure in throwing babies up in the air and practising shooting out their eyes – all in front of the parents of the children. Ulf Gorman, in his book *A Good God?*, claims that the same practice was followed by German soldiers in the Second World War.

These sort of examples need not be confined to the Russia of Ivan's day. In the second world war, the S.S. guards at Belsen and Treblinka used to save gas by throwing babies and young children into the gas chambers over the heads of the adults before shutting the doors. They would throw children under five, alive, into the bottom of the lime pits before throwing the dead bodies of those who had been gassed down on top of them. We need not look even as far afield as Germany – police reports in Britain indicate that up to twenty young children have been murdered whilst making "snuff" video films for paedophile viewers. Sexual abuse of young children is increasingly common with five- to seven-year-old girls being raped whilst young boy prostitutes on the streets of London command a higher price than their older sisters.

Ivan is claiming that, in Chisholm's terms, nothing can defeat or make worthwhile this suffering. The price is simply too high for any eventual state of happiness that may emerge.

The first response by traditional believers will be to say that God should not be blamed for such sufferings. These sufferings, they might say, are due to the actions of human beings and the Free Will Defence (which we looked at in chapter 3) explains why God could not intervene to prevent their occurrence. This, however, does not meet Ivan's point which is more subtle.

Ivan maintains that God, being omnipotent, omniscient and the creator of all must take final responsibility for everything that happens in the universe he created. God created the universe, he either knew what would happen (since traditional Christianity holds that God knows everything in the past, the present and the future) or he could predict with considerable accuracy those things that were likely to happen. In Genesis, God is recorded as looking at his creation and saying it is good. Ivan, by contrast, maintains that it is fundamentally flawed. The suffering of innocent children is simply too great a price to pay for any eventual state of bliss. If it was necessary for innocent children to suffer in this extreme way in order that God's ultimate ends should be brought about, then the means cannot justify the ends. It would have been better if the universe had never been created.

Ivan, therefore, accepts that God exists, but he does not accept God's world. He "returns his ticket", he refuses to play God's game. His brother, Alyosha, is devastated by Ivan's attack. Ivan asks him whether, had he been the architect of the world, he would have been willing to erect the whole of creation, if it was absolutely necessary for the little girl to suffer in the privy and Alyosha says No, he would not. Ivan also asks Alyosha what should be done with the Lord who had the young boy torn to bits in front of his parents and Alyosha says, "Kill him."

"Bravo! You're a fine hermit!" replies Ivan because even his holy brother agrees with his case and, indeed, Alyosha has no answer. Alyosha is appalled by Ivan's attack – particularly by the blasphemy of his attack on God. "This is rebellion," he says. "Rebellion? I am sorry to hear you say that," replies Ivan because he knows that one cannot live in rebellion against God. Ivan appreciates that God has all the cards, he has all the power and all Ivan can do is to protest and to reconcile himself to committing suicide in due course. He knows, of course, that God can punish him for his rebellion, but he considers that it is better to maintain his integrity and to live in rebellion and rejection of God than to submit in servile obedience to a power figure just because this power figure can exact punishment after death. Peter Geach argues that it is senseless or insane to defy an Almighty God, thus he says:

But what if somebody asks "Why should I obey God's laws?" This is really an insane question . . . A defiance of an Almighty God is insane (p.126). I shall be told . . . my attitude is plain power-worship. So it is: But it is worship of the Supreme power, and as such is wholly different from . . . a cringing attitude towards earthly powers.

(p.127)

Geach therefore distinguishes between obedience to earthly power figures on the grounds of their power, which he considers to be wrong, and obedience to the Supreme power figure which he considers to be right. Geach does not really argue in support of this position and Ivan would specifically reject it. Surely, Ivan might maintain, to obey a Supreme power figure because he can punish you is as unacceptable as obedience to any earthly power figure. Ivan stands in rebellion against God, whatever the consequences may be.

The question Ivan raises is one that few believers ever consider. Can the means God uses or allows possibly be justified by the end which God has in mind? The Free Will Defence maintains that it is necessary for God to allow evil in order that human beings should be free to enter into a love relationship with him. Ivan effectively rejects the FWD by claiming that the price of freedom is simply too high.

Jewish theologians sometimes accuse Christians of not taking suffering seriously enough and demand that any theology should be capable of being undertaken in the presence of burning children. In other words, if talk about God does not make sense in the presence of extreme suffering, then academic philosophers and theologians have no business getting involved in such talk. Ivan is making a similar demand and is effectively saying that the "bar-room games" of those who write about philosophy from the safety of universities in the Western world do not get near to addressing the reality or profundity of the problem of evil.

Is It All Worth It?

Theologians generally maintain that ends do not justify means. An example might illustrate this. Assume I have a sixteen-year-old daughter who is approached by a highly unattractive but wealthy old man who asks her to go to bed with him. She finds him repulsive but he says that, if she agrees, he will pay £100,000 to the charity of her choice. She is much concerned with the suffering in the Third World and knows that £100,000 could bring sight to ten thousand blind people or could educate and feed a hundred children for ten years, or could save the lives of a thousand people in a drought-stricken area. What, then, is she to do? Many would say that what she is being asked to do is evil and wicked and she should decline. However, the situation could be made more immediate. Assume that her brother had a rare disease and he could be flown to a hospital in the United States where an expensive operation is possible which would save his life – without the old man's money he would die. Should she agree to the old man's proposals to save her brother's life? If she should in this case, then Christianity maintains that those in the Third World should be regarded just as much as her brother as the boy with whom she has grown up.

Many Christians, of course, will still say that my daughter should not do this wicked thing, in spite of the good that would come of it. It is never permissible, they would hold, to do evil so that good may come. If, however, this is the position, then Ivan Karamazov's case becomes even stronger. If the ends can never justify the means, then surely the eventual ends that God has planned cannot justify the evil and suffering that takes place to innocent children? Better, Ivan would hold, for God never to have created the universe than to have created it as it is.

This is such an effective attack because it undermines any theodicy. God's actions in creating the world cannot be justified because of the suffering that has resulted. The price has simply been too high. It is important to remember that Ivan is attacking God as traditionally conceived. God is not held to be limited in his power which would enable him to be exonerated from blame for the existence of evil because he did the best he could in the circumstances. This would imply that "the circumstances" dictated what God could and could not do.

Assuming that God is omnipotent, then only if God was not omniscient and did not know what human beings would do with their freedom could he be exonerated. Even in this case, however, God must have known that extreme suffering inflicted by human beings on each other or by natural forces operating in the normal way were a strong possibility. Given this possibility, Ivan would hold, God should not have created the world as it is. The risk was simply too great.

To be sure, Ivan's attack appeals to the emotions. It asks us to be appalled at innocent suffering and to decide that nothing is worth the price. Some would argue that the eventual state of happiness for human beings in heaven is so great that any amount of suffering is worthwhile. This is equivalent to saying that the ends *can* justify the means if the ends are big enough or, to translate it into the example of my daughter, that it might be justified for her to go to bed with the old man if he paid a million pounds rather than a hundred thousand. Such an argument seems highly questionable.

Another approach would be to maintain that God has rights over us as owner and creator and has no obligation to us at all. God can, therefore, do with us as he wishes. As we saw in chapter 2, this would have been the theocentric approach adopted by Aquinas. However in the chapter on natural evil (chapter 4) this was questioned, and even if God considered that he had these rights, man may now be considered to have come of age and there seems no good reason why human beings should assent to the claims of their creator – there seems no good reason why Ivan or his followers should agree with God's position. The pot has grown to the state where it can question the potter and although the potter may not like being questioned, there seems no convincing argument why this should render the pot's approach invalid.

Of course, God has the power to destroy any human individuals.

However, if an individual fears being destroyed and acts on this basis, he is really giving in to force and is not taking a moral stand. Better, perhaps, to make a stand on principle no matter what the consequences, than to acquiesce in an immoral demand – so, at least, Ivan would claim. A guard in a concentration camp who took part in the slaughter of innocent gypsies, Communists, Poles, homosexuals and Jews because he was ordered to do so by the supreme power in his country, having been told that if he did not obey he would be shot, could hardly be considered to have acted morally. The defence of "obeying orders" was not held to justify many Nazis at the Nuremburg trials after the Second World War. Similarly Ivan might well argue that human beings should "return their ticket" to God, refusing to take part in his creation – no matter what the consequences.

If an individual does not consider Ivan's examples of the suffering of little children to be horrific in the extreme, then he or she may simply deny Ivan's approach – effectively saying, "What is all the fuss about? What is so very terrible about a small amount of human suffering?" I, for one, cannot accept this approach, although I agree that in rejecting it I am not doing so on the basis of philosophic argument so much as on the basis of a moral repugnance to accept anything which would willingly countenance the suffering of anyone, be they innocent children or adults. Ivan asks us whether *anything* can justify the extreme suffering of innocent children, whether it is the little girl locked in the privy and covered with her own excrement or the young children thrown alive into the lime pits at Auschwitz, Treblinka or Belsen. I cannot find it in me to say that this suffering can be justified by anything that I can imagine – but you, the reader, must make your own decision.

Summary

Ivan Karamazov maintains that the suffering of innocent children can never be justified by some eventual end or purpose planned by

God. He therefore rejects the world God has made, whilst accepting that the traditional God exists.

This approach undercuts the Free Will Defence as well as any attempt to explain natural evil, as it takes suffering really seriously and maintains that nothing is worth the price. It therefore rejects all attempts at theodicy. Each individual must decide for him- or herself whether this attack succeeds, but I do not think there is any rational answer to Ivan's challenge which could be sustained in the presence of burning children (which, after Auschwitz, seems a reasonable test for any theodicy).

SIX

Conclusion to the Problem of Evil

At the beginning of the first part of this book, we saw that the problem of evil arises because the believer maintains five premises:

1. God exists who created the universe from nothing,
2. This God continues to be interested in his creation,
3. God is good,
4. God is omnipotent,
5. God does not wish suffering to take place.

Anyone interested in a rational answer to the problem of evil needs to determine whether these propositions are compatible with the undoubted existence of extreme suffering and misery.

The main approaches that have traditionally been taken to the problem have been reviewed. We have considered what it means to talk of God's omnipotence and concluded that this is best defined as the ability of God to bring about any state of affairs which is absolutely possible and which does not go against his nature.

If we start with the facts in the world, it is difficult to arrive at the God to whom believers have traditionally regarded themselves as being committed. David Hume and John Stuart Mill both show that, starting from these facts and in the absence of any other assumptions, it is not possible to arrive at the all-powerful and wholly good God of Christian theism. The Thomist tradition (chapter 2) argues that this universe is good and perfect because it is made by the good and perfect God, and holds that we should look at the universe from a theocentric rather than an anthropocentric perspective. The Free Will Defence (chapter 3) seeks to show for what good reason God allows evil to occur and maintains that if individuals are to be truly free then God has no choice but to allow suffering to occur. Natural evil (chapter 4) can be explained by the need for natural laws to operate regularly and to provide the forum in which human beings learn to cope with their environment and to surmount the challenges with which they are faced, although the quantity of evil arising from natural forces seems difficult to justify.

All the potential explanations for the existence of evil have, however, to face the challenge put forward by Ivan Karamazov (chapter 5) – that the suffering of innocent children is simply not worth the price, no matter what glorious end God may have in view. Creation, on this view, is not good and Ivan accordingly rejects the world that God has made. He rebels against God.

Ivan's challenge is unable to show any logical incompatibility between the five propositions set out above and the existence of evil. There is no way of showing that it is logical nonsense to maintain belief in an omnipotent and wholly good God in the face of extreme suffering, but Ivan invites us to reject God on the basis of human compassion for those who suffer. This is not a logical disproof of God's existence nor is it logically conclusive, but the position is nevertheless persuasive – even though Ivan's rebellion is an intellectual response which does not involve him engaging with human suffering and trying to prevent it.

As a philosopher, I conclude that rationally and on balance Ivan's attack succeeds. I can see no way of defending the claim that the suffering of innocent children is worth any ultimate end, no matter how glorious. There seems no satisfactory argument why an omnipotent, omniscient and all-good God could not have created a world with less extreme suffering in it and if, for some unknown reason, the only basis on which this world could have been created was to allow hundreds of millions of children and adults to suffer and to die in agony of mind or body, then I have great sympathy with Ivan's rejection of the world God has made.

Conclusion to the Problem of Evil

The Free Will Defence seems to come closest to a justification for God's allowing suffering and evil to occur, but given the scale of the suffering and the pain it causes, Ivan Karamazov concludes that the price seems to be too high. Richard Swinburne would disagree, claiming that Ivan is asking for a "toy world" (*The Existence of God*, Oxford, p.oo) where nothing matters very much. As we have seen, Swinburne sees God's mercy in his setting limits to the amount human beings can suffer either by allowing human beings to faint when the pain passes a certain point or by claiming that death occurs after about seventy years. I have already said (chapter 5) that I consider this position to be obscene and to be one that could not be adopted by one who has lived in the presence of real suffering rather than contemplating it as an academic exercise.

Ivan's protest is reasonable and rationally justifiable. Stewart Sutherland's conclusion is that we should therefore dismiss belief in the traditional idea of God. He goes on (in *God, Jesus and Belief*, Blackwell, 1983) to develop an alternative way of understanding Christianity which may briefly be characterized as involving the individual seeking an ethical transcendence of self. Christian language is retained but the idea of a Creator God is dispensed with (I outline these ideas in *The Puzzle of God*).

The Revd Don Cupitt; Fr Gareth Moore O.P., Dewi Phillips and others have, in their different ways, developed revisionary views of Christianity which also do not require the traditional idea of God and these revisionary ideas are gaining support among clergy and some theologically aware lay people in both Catholic and Protestant Churches.

I do not accept the revisionary approaches to Christianity and in the second part of this book want to explore why, even though I agree with Sutherland about the effectiveness of Ivan Karamazov's attack, I end up with a radically different conclusion.

PART II

THE MYSTERY OF EVIL

Have you found your life distasteful?
My life did, and does, smack sweet.
Was your youth of pleasure wasteful?
Mine I saved and hold complete.
Did your joys with age diminish?
When mine fail me, I'll complain.
Must in death your daylight finish?
My sun rests to rise again.

ROBERT BROWNING

SEVEN

Introduction

Remember O Lord that your enemies laugh at you,
    that they are godless and despise you . . .
There is violence in every dark corner of the land . . .
Psalm 74:18, 20

In the first part of this book we saw that, if human reason is master, there seems to be no way of combining belief in an all-good and all-powerful God with the existence of extreme evil and suffering in the world. Because of this many have moved away from Christianity whilst others have sought to retain Christian language and practices whilst dismissing belief in a God who created the world and who sustains it and interacts with it.

One way out of this dilemma is to retreat behind mystery and to accept that God's ways are not our ways. The magnificent thirty-eighth to fortieth chapters of the book of Job take this approach and it is an attractive position. However, it is not one that many consider to be satisfactory in the face of the hideous suffering of which we are now routinely aware.

In the second half of this book, I want to argue for an alternative approach. I do not want to deny the importance of human reason nor the need to search and probe intellectually this most thorny of all theological problems – however, I want to take as my starting point St Augustine's statement:

Credo ut intelligam.

or

I believe in order that I may understand.

I know of no adequate basis by which the existence of God can be proved from premises that do not somehow include the conclusion. In other words, if one starts out with opening assumptions that do not include the existence of God, I know of no ways in which the existence of God can be proved or even made more probable than not (I review the main arguments for the existence of God in *The Puzzle of God*, (HarperCollins, 1990). Basil Mitchell (*The Justification of Religious Belief*) and Richard Swinburne (*The Existence of God*) have attempted to put forward a cumulative case and a probability approach for God's existence but in the assessment of probability much depends on an individual's presuppositions – some people will accept the key presuppositions on which the arguments rest and some will not. Those that do accept them will be convinced the arguments succeed but those that reject the presuppositions will reject the arguments. There seems an unbridgeable gap between the two. G. K. Chesterton recognized this when he said: "You will sooner catch Leviathan with a hook than convert a soul on a syllogism." Debates about the arguments for and against God's existence are interminable simply because they rest on key assumptions and these assumptions cannot themselves be justified.

St Augustine did not believe that God's existence could be proved – instead he started with faith. As Tertullian said: "What has Athens to do with Jerusalem?" Athens was the city of the philosophers, Jerusalem the city of faith and the two were not connected. However, Augustine, once he had faith, then used his intellect to try to understand theological and philosophical problems. I am going to take this approach in this part of the book. In other words I am going to take the existence of the traditional Christian idea of God as given and then work from this starting point.

A prerequisite of this approach is, of course, some minimal definition of God which will have to be unpacked in the pages which follow. The definition I am working with is that God can correctly be described as personal and loving, who is three persons in one and who is the creator and sustainer of the universe, who interacts with his creation and who calls human beings to respond to him in love both for himself and for each other. For the avoidance of doubt, I maintain that language about this God is correctly used in a realist sense – in other words "God exists" is true if and only if there exists a God independent of the universe, of human language, the human community or the human psyche, who can correctly be described in the terms I have here set out.

The problems that need to be tackled if this second half of the book is to be at all useful include the following:

Given that God exists:

1. What does it mean to describe God as good?
2. What does it mean to describe God as Almighty?
3. How can it be morally justifiable to hold that God acts selectively within the world when in so many cases where real evil occurs there appears to be no such action?
4. What explanation can be given for the existence of physical evils?
5. How can extreme suffering of innocents be justified?
6. What does it mean to talk of the Devil?
7. What does it mean to say that human beings are free?

This is a tall agenda to be tackled in half a book! Nevertheless I believe it is possible given the ground covered in the first half – to which I shall be referring. My aim is not to solve the problems with which the first half concluded – I have already said that I do not think this can be done. My aim is more modest. It is to outline as persuasive a position as possible that could be taken by the person with faith in the traditional idea of God when confronted with the reality of evil and suffering. The non-believer will be readily able to reject many of the arguments as they all begin with the existence of God as a starting point. Augustine's insight here is, I believe, sound – that the person who believes in God will have a different understanding from the person who does not. Which of the two is right will depend on whether or not God exists.

At the outset, I do not claim that the account given here is the right one. My hope, however, is that it may be persuasive to those who share the traditional Christian faith. To claim to understand the ways of God would be presumptive folly. However, the difficulty of understanding God does not mean that, in the face of extreme suffering, the attempt must not be made to face up to the reality of evil. We must wrestle with the problem, however difficult it may be.

As we go through the second half of this book, we will build up a series of statements which I will argue expresses the central Christian convictions in relation to the problem of evil. We can start with the first statement. The believer may start by saying:

i) I accept the existence of a creator God as previously defined.

This, however, is only the beginning.

EIGHT

The Euthyphro Dilemma

Give thanks to the Lord, because he is good.
Psalm 107:1

We have to immediately address a relatively difficult area – it concerns the nature of morality and what it means to say that God is good. This is one of the key assumptions on which the problem of evil depends.

What is the basis for actions being good and evil? The Divine Command Theory of ethics, in its basic form, assumes that:

1. If it is against God's will for me to do X, then
2. It is wrong for me to do X.

On this basis, it is logically possible for God to command that people should perform vicious acts for their own sake alone and not for any external reason. William Ockham maintained that acts which we would label "theft" or "adultery" would be right if they were commanded by God. This is perfectly correct on the basis of the Divine Command Theory of ethics. By contrast, modern morality finds little place for God and rejects the idea that God's wishes have any part to play in morality. The argument against God's involvement is outlined by Peter Geach:

> If what God commands is *not* right, then the fact of his commanding it is no moral reason for obedience though it may in that case be dangerous to disobey. And if what God commands *is* right, even so it is not God's commanding it that makes it right;

on the contrary, God as a moral being could command only what was right apart from his commanding it. So God has no essential place in the foundations of morality.

(from "The moral law and the law of God"
in Paul Helm's *Divine Commands and Morality*)

Duns Scotus supported this view and rejected the Divine Command Theory of ethics saying that what is good or bad is independent of God's wishes, but God's commands provide the moral obligation for us to act in accordance with the good. In other words, we should do what is good or bad because God commands us – even though what is good or bad is not dependent on God.

This argument is not new. It originated in Plato's *Euthyphro* in which Socrates is in discussion with a young Athenian gentleman, Euthyphro. The discussion proceeds as follows:

Euthyphro and Socrates are discussing the trial in which Euthyphro is to appear as the prosecutor of his own father. One peasant killed another in a drunken fight and Euthyphro's father had tied up the killer, notified the authorities, thrown him into a ditch and forgotten about him. The killer died of cold and hunger whilst in the ditch. Euthyphro was concerned that the gods might punish him if he had dinner with his father who had done this, so he felt obliged to put matters right by prosecuting his father.

Socrates is outraged that Euthyphro should prosecute his own father over the death of an insignificant peasant whose death was of no importance to anyone. He asks Euthyphro whether good deeds are good because they please the gods, or whether they please the gods because they are good deeds. In spite of Socrates' various arguments, Euthyphro is not convinced – he does not reply with philosophic arguments but asserts that it does not really matter who was the murderer, what relationship he has to the person prosecuting or whether the victim was a peasant. All that matters is whether a man was done to death in a manner which all the gods must hate. Euthyphro claims that the wishes of the gods decide morality – and he must obey these wishes.

The discussion ends with Euthyphro declining to go on with the debate due to lack of time. He leaves to go about his business and the reader is left feeling that Socrates has won the argument philosophically, but Euthyphro is sticking to his position in spite of this. It appears like convincing philosophic argument against simple faith. Euthyphro certainly was not taking a position that was likely to make him popular – Athenian courts would be unlikely to be impressed by the death of a peasant who would be considered of little worth. Nevertheless Euthyphro feels compelled to act as he does out of "fear of the gods".

The issue is whether divine commands determine what is right or wrong and good or bad or whether morality can judge Divine Commands. Which, in other words, is supreme – the wishes of God or some independent standard? If these two conflict, who should be allowed the mastery? Is there a separate realm of morals independent of God?

In a way, the Platonic idea of the Forms is central to the discussion. Plato considered that everything in time and space, in other words the whole of the universe, was imperfect. The world as we see it is but a pale shadow of the true timeless and spaceless reality.

For Plato, instances of beauty, truth, justice or goodness which we see here on earth participate in the perfect and changeless Forms which represent real or pure Beauty, Truth, Justice and Goodness. This pure reality is the realm of the Forms (it is worth noticing that the Forms are, by convention, referred to with a capital letter – so instances of justice participate in or partially resemble the timeless and spaceless Form of Justice).

Plato's God, the Demiurge, did not create the universe from nothing. Instead it appears that he used pre-existing material to fashion the temporal and spatial universe using the Forms as a model. Inevitably there would be imperfections in this universe – firstly because the pre-existent matter from which it was formed was flawed and also because, for Plato, true perfection had to be beyond time and space (since anything in time would either be getting better, in which case it was not already perfect, or it would be getting worse, in which case it was not perfect either).

Applying this to morality, Plato thought that the perfect Forms of Goodness, Justice, Virtue, etc. existed independently of God. There was, therefore, a standard against which God's wishes could be measured. It is for this reason that Plato has Socrates (in *Euthyphro*) argue against Euthyphro's view that morality was just based on divine commands.

However most people today reject Plato's idea of the Forms. The Bible, also, has no such idea. God is to be obeyed because He is God. God's word is law. Divine commands are just and right because they are divine commands, not because they are measured against some external standard. The Ten Commandments given to Moses are to be followed because they represent the Law given by God – the Israelites are not called to exercise their reason to determine whether or not what God commands is really good.

Whichever horn of the Euthyphro dilemma is taken gives rise to difficulties. If one adopts the Divine Command Theory of ethics, then what is good depends on what God commands, just because God commands it. There is no way of judging God to be good or bad, since what is good is whatever God wants. There is no independent standpoint against which to measure or judge God. The very idea of goodness depends on God's will.

The problem then arises as to why anyone should worship God. Some might say that one should worship because of God's power. This, however, is a poor reason. Anyone who obeyed another because of their power is not acting morally or rationally. In the Second World War, the German government was undoubtedly powerful, but this was no reason why, morally, concentration camps should be tolerated simply because the government ordered their creation. In this case, we claim that there is a higher ideal of justice and right conduct to which appeal can be made and which rendered any order by the Nazi government to massacre Jews, Poles, Communists, gypsies and homosexuals unacceptable. It could not be morally right to obey Hitler just because Hitler had total power in Germany. Similarly it may be held that it cannot be morally right to worship God if the only reason for doing so is that God is more powerful than any other force. The result is that if we take Euthyphro's side in his argument against Socrates, then we are left wondering why God should be worshipped.

If one rejects this approach and claims that God should be worshipped because he is good then other difficulties arise. If I say that my son is good, then this is a judgement about him. I measure his behaviour against external standards and judge, by reference to these standards, that he deserves the accolade "good".

If goodness is given as a reason for worshipping God, then it means that we are judging God against a standard of goodness that is independent of him. Thus saying "My son is good" and "God is good" would have the same logical structure – we would be judging both my son and God against an independent standard. On this view it would make sense to question whether, in fact, God was good. We could, for instance, look at his action in history, as recorded in the Bible, and come to the conclusion that God was not good. If, however, God *was* considered as good, then this would indeed be a reason for worshipping him. God could be distinguished from Satan because God is good and Satan is bad, where "good" and "bad" refer to independent standards against which both God and Satan could be measured.

If, therefore, we take Socrates' side of the argument, in his discussion with Euthyphro, we will want to claim that there is a standard of goodness independent of God – possibly (although not necessarily) like Plato's Forms.

The debate between these two positions is still very much alive, and the consequences are important. Central to consideration of the problem of evil, as we have seen in chapter 1, is the statement that

"God is good". If we are willing to say that God's goodness can include him not objecting to the extreme suffering of humans and animals in his creation, then evil can be blamed directly on God's action, and the existence of evil is no longer an intellectual problem as God is directly responsible. However most believers do not want to say this – they wish to maintain that "God is good" means that God is opposed to evil and suffering.

One factor to be considered in determining which side of the Euthyphro dilemma to hold, is whether God is a moral agent. Does God, in other words, choose between alternatives? Much depends on whether God is inside or outside time.

If God is literally timeless and spaceless (the view held by St Augustine and St Thomas Aquinas as well as many Roman Catholic theologians), then God is totally unchanging in a very strong sense. He *cannot* be other than he is. He is totally simple and completely perfect. There is one single act of God and all time – past, present and future – is equally present to him in one simultaneous instant. Hannibal's crossing the Alps, your birth and the end of the world are all simultaneously present to the timeless God. Such a God is not a moral agent. He does not choose or deliberate between alternatives. In his one perfect timeless act, the timeless God timelessly brings about effects which occur at different moments in our time. If "God is good" is analytic, everything the timeless God does is good because, by definition, whatever the timeless God does is what is called good.

Aquinas took a slightly different view, although he worked with a model of God as timeless. Good, for Aquinas, is "that to which all desire tends" (he took this idea from Aristotle who, in the *Nichomachean Ethics* suggested that the good was "that at which all things aim"). To name God as good is, therefore, to name him as the goal of all desire. Goodness is that which is desirable and attractive, it is that to which all things are drawn, even though we may not be clear what this goodness amounts to in the case of God.

For Aristotle, and for Aquinas after him, something is good insofar as it has succeeded in being what, by its nature, it is intended to be. Since God is literally timeless and unchanging, God is always fully whatever it is to be God. God is "pure actuality", God has no potential at all. God is, therefore, supremely good.

Aquinas, therefore, held two positions: "God is good" is analytically true in that, by his definition, God is fully whatever it is to be God and is therefore necessarily good because of this. However "God is good" is also synthetic to the extent that we are saying that "God is that to which all desire tends". This is to give a reason for obeying God's commands, as it is logical to obey the commands of God once one has accepted that all desire tends towards God.

God, on Aquinas' view, is not a "good being or thing", since God is *not* either a being or thing. We cannot know what God, as ineffable, unknowable substance, is, but we can know that, whatever it is to be God, God is fully that. Since God creates everything and everything depends on God, God is the goal and aim of all creation – whether they realize this or not.

It may, of course, be argued that all human desire does *not* tend to God. Most of the human race are concerned with their day-to-day needs, their family and happiness. Aquinas might reply to this by saying that God is the goal to which all desires *should* tend if they were enlightened, but, again, there may be individuals who would question this. It smacks of an assumption.

If, on the other hand, God is everlasting, without beginning and without end (the view held by most Protestant theologians although some Roman Catholics as well) then, although God is unchanging in his love and care for his creation, time does pass for him. A thousand ages in his sight may be but an evening gone, but the evening has still gone. God is an everlasting spirit who acts and reacts with the universe he has created and sustains. On this view, God's actions and their effects both take place in time. The future is future to God, although, of course, God's knowledge of the future is much greater than ours as his knowledge of the present is so much greater than ours. On this view, God is indeed a moral agent – a personal

God able to make choices between different alternatives. On this view, "God is good" may either express a judgement about God against an independent standard of morality or it may express the conviction that all moral standards depend on God's wishes. There are, as we have seen, problems in both cases.

Both horns of the Euthyphro dilemma depend on the assumption that there are some absolute standards of morality – the debate is about whether or not these absolute standards depend on God's wishes. An alternative is to hold that there are no absolutes – morality is relative to different societies and social systems and varies over time. Thus three thousand years ago it was considered wrong to eat pork because of the health hazards in hot countries just as it was considered wrong to lend money at interest – today many people eat pork sausages and have building society accounts (although even today Muslims will resist charging or receiving interest on money). In China it is bad to have more than one child, because this is socially unacceptable. In Turkey, it is good. Morality, then, may be held to be essentially relative between different societies. If we take this view, then both horns of the Euthyphro dilemma may be rejected as morality *neither* depends on what God wants *nor* depends on some independent standard. Instead, morality is a human construct which is adapted and changed by the societies in which we live to meet different conditions.

We are faced with the situation, therefore, that it is far from clear what it means to say that "God is good", yet we need to be clear on what this means if we are to make sense of the problem of evil. David Hume held that a God who was all-powerful and did not eliminate evil must be malevolent, so when the believer says that God is good he or she needs to give some content to this claim. In the next chapter I want to suggest an alternative way of approaching the problem by using the thought of a neglected nineteenth-century theologian and philosopher, Albrecht Ritschl.

Summary

If there is a God and if God is held to be good, then this can apparently mean one of two things. Either God's actions and character are good when measured against some independent standard, and in this case there is something independent of God against which God can be judged which may be held to diminish him, or God is his own standard of goodness – whatever God wants is good just because he wants it. In this case God seems to be a power figure. Both positions give rise to very real problems.

For the believer who is faced by the problem of evil and suffering, it is important to understand what it means to talk of God's goodness. In the next chapter, a way will be suggested of understanding this claim about God which avoids both horns of the Euthyphro dilemma.

NINE

Albrecht Ritschl – Absolute Value Judgements

> The Lord is great and to be highly praised;
>   His greatness is beyond understanding . . .
> People will tell about all your goodness
>   and sing about your kindness . . .
> The Lord is good . . .
>
> Psalm 145: 3, 7, 9

In the previous chapter we saw that analysis of the Euthyphro dilemma shows that there are problems both with saying that morality depends on God so that God is the only arbiter of what is good and with the view that there is a standard of goodness independent of God. I want to suggest an alternative view, which denies there are any clear moral absolutes at all. The whole Euthyphro dilemma rests on the assumption that such moral absolutes exist – if this is denied, then there is no problem remaining.

Consider possible responses to moral questions such as:

– Why should I not kill?
– Why should I not steal?
– Why should I not commit adultery?
– Why should I not be unemployed if I wish?

These questions may be answered in various ways, but a distinction needs to be made between two types of answer:

1. Where reasons are given why I should not act in a certain way. The questions appear to expect some such answer – thus the question

about being unemployed may be answered by reference to the importance of work to the community, the wrongness of living off the state when there is no alternative, the corrosive effect of unemployment on the individual and so on. Each of these questions could, in turn, be further debated and further "Why?" questions posed.

2. Where a questioner is simply told to act in accordance with his duty. Thus "It is a duty to work." This appeal to duty derives from Kant. If someone asks "Why?", then the answer would tend to be circular and to come back to a simple statement of what the person's duty is. Churches are sometimes good at this: "It is a duty to go to Mass", "to go to Confession", etc., with few, if any, reasons being given.

An authoritarian body, state or Church can make all sorts of things a duty from burning heretics, to exposing witches, to wearing the traditional woman's black *chadou*, to killing Jews, to condemning certain books or certain actions. *If acting from a sense of duty is the highest path, then murder or theft committed in accordance with a sense of duty may be held to be virtuous.* The Ayatollah Khomeini made it a holy duty to kill the author, Salman Rushdie, assuring Muslims that anyone who carried out this act would go straight to heaven as well as receiving a very substantial financial reward if they survived the murder. Here we have a religious duty supposedly transforming what most people would consider to be an evil and wicked act into a supposedly holy obligation.

The appeal to duty is a powerful appeal, but not a rational one. Countries expect their sons and daughters to fight and die from a sense of duty, but do not give reasons. To explain to a Russian soldier why he should have died in Afghanistan, to an American why he should have died in Vietnam, to a Briton or German why he should have died in the First World War, etc. would be quite a tall order and argument would inevitably include assumptions which he might not accept.

Appeal to reason seems, therefore, the preferable course, but most rational appeals get one involved in a regress of justification. Thus if we take the question "Why should I not commit murder?", one could imagine answers such as:

- Murder involves killing another human being.
- No society could exist where anyone was allowed to kill others.
- Society is necessary as human beings need to live together.
- It is important that human beings live together and prosper.

At some stage one is going to come to a value judgement that is not justified in terms of an antecedent position. Almost everyone would accept the last of the above statements but it cannot be proved to be true – it is a judgement that almost everyone would accept.

It is worth here referring back to a nineteenth-century theologian, Albrecht Ritschl, whose writings today are almost totally ignored. Ritschl was born in 1822 and was influenced by Baur and the Tübingen school in Germany. The Tübingen school were at the forefront of new methods of biblical exegesis, but Ritschl's concerns were more with the grounding of religious belief. He had two aims:

1. To justify religious belief and to give it a pragmatic basis, and
2. To establish the unique identity of Christianity.

Ritschl believed that there had to be a total separation of religion and theoretical knowledge. One could not reason one's way to God. This move away from theoretical knowledge was a move away from the idea, common in the nineteenth century, that religion gave the only adequate answer to the universe.

Ritschl laid great stress on the historic truth of Christianity. Fundamental to Ritschl was the distinction between man as a part of the physical universe and man as a spiritual personality. This contradiction, he considered, could only be resolved through faith. Ritschl's view is a relevant one today as many modern theologians

consider that human beings find themselves in a position of contradiction. Niebuhr in his Gifford lectures had the same starting point as Ritschl, that man is in a position of contradiction.

Ritschl considered that what man seeks in religion is the attainment of a personal good. He regarded Christianity as pre-eminent because it stresses the individual and the personal character of Christ. What matters is the impact of Christ on our lives. Ritschl believed in a personal God and he considered that religion was grounded in man as a personal moral agent.

Rational arguments, he maintained, cannot prove the existence of God. (In chapter 7 I said that, following St Augustine, I agreed with this position.) Christianity is about a series of value judgements by the individual. Value judgements are not susceptible to proof, although they convey truth which is intuitive. The truth of value judgements is self-authenticating – although, of course, the person making such a value judgement has to accept the possibility that he or she could be wrong. It is important here to be clear that Ritschl is not saying that human beings make judgements about the world and then choose to live by them. Don Cupitt in his book *What is a Story?* (SCM Press, 1991), says that all religious stories are fictions and the Christian is the person who chooses to live by the fictional Christian story. This is not Ritschl's position. Ritschl considered the Christian story to be absolutely true – but held that it could only be recognized as true by an individual making a personal commitment to it in the form of a value judgement. This value judgement is not simply academic but involves the commitment of the individual's whole life. On this basis, when individuals say that God is good they are committing themselves to a view about the purpose and meaning of human existence. They may hold that God created human beings and human beings are made for God – this is their destiny and their purpose in existing. Of course, because this value judgement cannot be proved it could be mistaken, but that is the risk that faith has to run.

Unless the value judgements work themselves out in practical terms, which means in terms of actions in accordance with the second commandment, they will be bogus. So Christian faith cannot be egotistical and selfish. Philosophical views are useless as they fail to express God's importance for men as sinners and they omit the crucial elements of forgiveness and reconciliation.

For Ritschl, the central value judgement must be the dependence of man on God and of the individual on his personal relationship with God. For Kant, morality is at the centre – not so for Ritschl. The religious person marches to a different drummer and operates with a different supreme value judgement – the first commandment:

Thou shalt love the Lord thy God with all thy heart, and with all thy soul and with all thy mind and him only shalt thou serve.

The significance of the first commandment is often overlooked today, and Christianity becomes too concerned with the second – with the view that one should "Love one's neighbour as oneself". However, the second commandment *is* second, the first is primary. This can provide a key to unlocking almost every moral door, but *not* by reference to absolute moral laws laid down by God. The idea of absolute moral laws are, in any case, very difficult to get off the ground (try to think of *one* absolute moral law that cannot have an exception in unusual circumstances!). The best might be:

Do not commit murder of innocent children.

But, of course, someone who wanted to kill children would say that what they are doing is not murder or that the children were not innocent. For instance, a helicopter pilot dropping napalm on villages in Vietnam would not see himself as "murdering innocent children", but as "defending freedom". Similarly someone who believes that birth control is wrong and who insists that a poor woman in the Third World whose husband forces her to sleep with him from time to time should not practise birth control is "preserving the sanctity of the marriage relationship" rather than "contributing to malnutrition,

starvation, despair and death" for the woman's other twelve children.

The primacy of the first commandment means that *the individual places God at the centre of his priorities* and measures all his actions in the light of the first commandment. Of course, there are problems with this. Either:

1. One adopts the view that one has a personal relationship with God and therefore the individual places his or her relationship with God in the centre of his or her life, deciding in the light of this relationship and in the light of what he or she knows of God through the Bible, the Church and his or her fellows what actions would or would not be in accordance with the first commandment (this is the more Protestant view), or

2. The individual relies primarily on the teaching and guidance of the Church tradition (this is the approach normally taken by the Roman Catholic Church).

The danger of the first alternative is that too much may be left to individual intuition and there may be no ways of validating a claimed "duty to God" – this can lead to individuals acting against the good of others and taking up extreme and harmful positions because they believe themselves to have been called to do so by the deity.

The danger of the second alternative is that it may mean a move back to the "duty" option with obedience to the Church being seen as paramount and "My Church right or wrong" being the mainspring of conduct. The view taken may also be on the boundary lines between the two positions. Some people may obey the commands of their Church without thinking issues through for themselves and others will take the teaching of the Church not as obligatory commands but as indicators which should be taken seriously but which must nevertheless be judged by the individual in the light of his or her own personal relationship with God.

Ritschl's approach does not mean adopting either horn of the

Euthyphro dilemma. Certainly no standard external to God is being affirmed – the believer is not measuring God against any independent, transcendent ethic. The believer is also not straightforwardly accepting a Divine Command Theory of ethics, he or she may well consider that most moral codes are human constructs designed to help people live together in relative peace and harmony. However by naming God as good the believer is making the ultimate claim that God is the only proper and real end of all human striving – that God is the ultimate source of everything that we regard as good in this world.

A similar point is made (without referring to Ritschl) by the Swedish philosopher Ulf Gorman in his book *A good God?* (published by Verbum, Hakan Ohlssons, 1977). Gorman considers that:

> The problem of evil, then, is not a question concerning the existence of a certain supernatural being, but instead a question concerning the goodness of such a being: Is it reasonable to consider God as good in an evaluative sense, given the criteria of goodness considered to explain evil in the world? To answer this question is to make an evaluative commitment which has moral implications.
>
> (p.149)

Believers thus make a value judgement (Gorman terms it an "evaluative commitment") which places God at the centre of their lives, and emphasize their claim that it is in God that the summit of truth, goodness and justice is found. Believers may well seek to discern God's will, possibly through a process of discernment rather like that suggested by St Ignatius of Loyola in his Spiritual Exercises – which form the key to Jesuit spirituality. Ignatius envisages the individual going through a prolonged process of discernment to seek God's will and can be interpreted as maintaining that, in the final analysis, it is the individual's conscience that must reign supreme, not the dictates of the Church, although obviously such teaching will be taken seriously as part of the overall discernment process.

We saw in the last chapter that, for Aquinas, God was "that to which all desire tends". To name God as good is, therefore, to name him as the goal of all desire. This has similarities with Ritschl's approach. The believer stakes his or her life on the absolute value judgement that God is the ultimate end for human beings and thus calls God good. The non-believer, naturally, disagrees as he or she makes a different value judgement.

To call God good is, therefore, to be making a realist truth claim. It is to claim that the statement "God is good" is true because a relationship with the creator God which shows forth in a life of love of those around us is the only truly fulfilling goal for human beings. However there may be a variety of moral codes that can contribute to human flourishing and they may all be able to help to bring a person closer to God. Being a realist about the claim that "God is good" (in other words claiming that this is something we *discover*, not something created or made up within a particular society) does not necessarily mean that one is committed to saying that there is only one "right" moral system. One can be an anti-realist about morals, maintaining that moral truths rest on coherence within a particular society or form of life, but this does not prevent one being a realist about "God is good".

This distinction between changing moral systems and the absolute aim for human beings of drawing closer to God is important as it overcomes the problem faced by many who wish to be realists about God and about the claim that God is good but who are challenged by those who maintain that morality is relative to different societies and different ages. Morality almost certainly is relative. Moral situations change and much depends on the context from which moral dilemmas are viewed. Eating pork may well have been seen as morally wrong in a hot, Mediterranean country with no refrigeration; having more than one child may well be considered to be morally wrong in overcrowded India or China; sex before marriage, even as part of a long-term loving relationship, may well have been wrong where there were no reliable methods of birth control and where descent was the key to property rights – but situations change.

Moral systems can, therefore, be allowed to be relative to different times and places but they can all be seen as fostering human flourishing – and one can be a realist about this. The only real and worthwhile end for human beings, the only end in which men and women can find peace, contentment, meaning and value may be held to be in relation with the living God and it is this that is being affirmed when the believer names God as good. He or she is making the ultimate value judgement which is held to be true because only God provides the true end for human striving. Evil, on this basis, is anything which hinders, retards or prevents this ultimate endeavour, which gets in the way of individuals coming to be aware of God and living their lives so that they can become more like what they are intended to be. On this view, evil can take many and diverse forms, but all the forms seek to separate the individual from God.

The believer can express his or her position so far by affirming the following statements:

i) I accept the existence of a creator God as previously defined.

ii) I make a supreme value judgement by which I hold that the ultimate purpose and meaning for human existence is to be found only in fellowship with and love of God and living out this love in a life of self-giving love to those around us. For this reason I call God good as God is the ultimate source of everything I value most highly. Evil represents anything that makes it more difficult for individuals to achieve this purpose.

Summary

To call God good is to express the fundamental value judgement made by the believer in which he or she affirms that God is the only worthwhile goal for all human striving. A person who holds this view may accept that moral systems are man-made and relative but may consider that different moral systems may draw people closer to God. There may be a variety of paths, but there is only a single destination. Evil takes many forms, but covers all those things which hinder human beings achieving the destiny for which they are intended.

TEN

God Almighty

O Lord my God how great you are!
You have spread out the heavens like a tent . . .
You have set the earth firmly on its foundations . . .
Lord, you made so many things!
How wisely you made them all!

Psalm 104:1, 2b, 5, 24

God is traditionally held to be omnipotent, yet if God can do everything why does he not abolish all the evil and suffering in the world?

Many definitions have been given as to what it means to talk of God being omnipotent. The most extreme is that of Descartes – that God can do anything at all, even the logically impossible (see chapter 2). God could, on this view, make a square circle; make a stone too heavy for him to lift – and then go on to lift it; make unbreakable promises, and then break them and even swear by a being greater than himself and so on. This is not a serious candidate as once one abandons the law of non-contradiction, one lapses into nonsense. It is no limitation on God to say that he could not make a square circle. A square circle is nonsensical – it is logical nonsense since anything that is a square cannot be a circle and vice versa. Of course God might make some obscure figure and call this a square circle, but then this would not be a square and a circle as we understand these terms.

More important, a God who could literally do anything at all would be a God who could eliminate all evil and suffering without in any way interfering with human freedom – he could actualize what

Ninian Smart calls "The Utopia Thesis" (which was discussed in chapter 3). God could do the logically impossible, he could make a world in which no-one ever suffered, no-one was ever depressed, no-one was ever hurt or died and yet everything else stayed exactly the same. God's failure to take this option could only mean that he was malevolent. The Utopian Thesis is as much logical nonsense as is the idea of a square circle – if human beings are to be genuinely free then they cannot be *made* to be always good.

God's omnipotence is sometimes held to be the power to do anything that is logically possible. However even this is not satisfactory as it is certainly logically possible for me to be able to swim, to sin or to commit suicide. God, however, having no body, being perfectly good and unchanging, cannot do these things.

The most plausible definition of God's omnipotence, although it still has a number of problems, is that put forward by Anthony Kenny (*The God of the Philosophers*). Kenny first gives a general definition of omnipotence:

> X is omnipotent iff X is capable of performing any action A such that the proposition "X performs A" is logically possible. ("iff" here means "if and only if")

Kenny rejects this definition because he maintains that it could also be applied to a human being who had very limited capacities and he therefore substitutes a definition more specifically related to God:

> The possession of all logically possible powers which it is possible for a being with the attributes of God to possess.

Kenny concentrates on "possible powers" rather than "possible actions" which God can perform and this is helpful. On this basis God cannot commit suicide, as this would mean going out of existence and this would be against his nature; God cannot sin, as this would mean him being less than perfect; and cannot swim, as this would entail him having a body. It permits God to have all the powers that it is logically possible for a being with the nature of God to have. God, then, cannot go against his own nature.

This idea of God as a supreme power figure has been very important in Christian theology. It is not, however, a strictly biblical idea, rather it came from the Greek philosophic idea of God's insurpassibility combined with the view of some early Church Fathers that God should not in any way be limited by lack of power. God should be able to do anything he wished in the world. On the face of it this seems to be obviously true. God, if he is to be God, must be able to do anything at all. This was part of the point of the miracle of Jesus turning water into wine and also his walking on water – to show that he had power over the physical elements. God's providential care of his people, therefore, cannot be held to be limited by lack of power.

Aquinas maintained that God was literally timeless but, although outside time, he was nevertheless omniscient and omnipotent. God was in complete charge of the whole of his creation and brought his purposes about in this world as he decreed. God's providence governed all things and the whole of life was in the hands of God. No theologian seriously challenged this view. It has been endorsed uniformly by Catholic theologians and both Luther and Calvin strongly supported it. They all accepted that God's providence governed all.

However, what it means to talk of God's providence is much more complicated than first appears. Certainly God's sustaining care maintains the universe in existence and he sends the rain on the just and the unjust (Matthew 5:45). Every person, creature and part of creation is dependent on God. This does not necessarily mean, however, that God is in full control of history and of the day-to-day details of human lives. God numbers every hair of the disciples' heads. In other words he is omniscient and knows all that happens. However, numbering of each hair is not the same as bringing about when each hair will fall out! If theologians seriously wish to claim that every event in the world is brought about by God then firstly there are major problems with human freedom and secondly God's responsibility for the suffering in the world becomes very great.

I want to argue that a much more restricted view of God's omnipotence is required and that one of the major reasons that Christians have intellectual difficulties in believing in God in the face of the evil in the world is that they have a too exalted view of God's power. God's power is much more limited than is generally supposed and, far from this restricting God, it actually places him in his proper place.

Christian attitudes to the Bible differ. Some hold that the Bible is the literal word of God and must be read as such. Others hold that interpretation is required – either by the individual or in the light of the tradition of their Church. Almost all Christians, however, maintain that the Bible forms a central part of their faith and any approach to the problem of evil that does not at least consider the biblical viewpoint is suspect. Generally, philosophers have ignored what the Bible has to say on the subject.

An omnipotent being who could accomplish anything by his word alone would be in total control of the world – yet the Old Testament gives us the picture of a world at least partly outside God's control. God continually has to intervene in order to meet the situations caused by the sin and error of the people of Israel. God's control is exercised by continual intervention to remedy the problems caused by the sin of his chosen people. At times Yahweh has to take extreme steps. For instance in Genesis 6:5–7:

> When the Lord saw how wicked everyone on earth was and how evil their thoughts were all the time, he was sorry that he had ever made them and put them on the earth. He was so filled with regret that he said: "I will wipe out these people I have created, and also the animals and the birds, because I am sorry that I made any of them."

At other times, God uses war as an instrument to bring about his intention, either by using the armies of Israel and aiding them or else by using the armies of Israel's enemies to punish his people (e.g. Jeremiah 22:24–30 and Ezekiel 38). God rarely acts directly. He works through the principle of "double agency" whereby God works through human agents and this is seen as normative in the Old Testament.

God works through "Salvation History". For instance, Yahweh calls Abraham out from Ur of the Chaldees, he cares for Jacob, he brings the people of Israel out of their slavery in Egypt, he helps them to take control of the land of Canaan, he uses the Babylonians to destroy the Temple in Jerusalem and the nation of Israel because of the wickedness of his chosen people and has the remnant carried off to slavery, he then restores their descendants to their land and arranges for them to be helped to rebuild the Temple and he sets up King David and his line through which his long-term purposes will be fulfilled. Always, however, God has to act to bring his purposes about. Almost always his action is mediated – in other words he acts through kings, rulers and individuals to bring his purposes about, even when they do not know they are carrying out God's intentions.

This idea of God being in control of human history is far less pronounced in the New Testament than in the Old. In fact, one of the things that makes the New Testament distinctive is that God's role in history is played down. We find no reference at all in the New Testament to God acting through the Roman soldiers who occupy Israel; no reference to God punishing Israel through the actions of the occupying troops; no predictions, so common in the Old, that the God of battles will defend Israel and restore her independence. The shift in perspective is massive, yet has not really been considered by most theologians.

In the Gospels, God is not portrayed as being in control of the world. He is able to act selectively, but his powers are severely limited and he acts through people. The magnificent first chapter of St John's Gospel, the most theological of the four Gospels, starts as follows:

God Almighty

> In the beginning was the Word, and the Word was with God,
>   and the Word was God.
> The same was in the beginning with God.
> All things were made by him, and without him was not anything
>   made that was made.
> In him was life; and the life was the light of men.
> And the light shineth in the darkness and the darkness
>   comprehended it not.

(John 1:1-5, Authorized Version)

The images from this passage have been overused and we have become so familiar with them that their meaning has almost become disregarded. This passage makes clear that everything was made by God and that the Word is life and light. The life is light for human beings and the light shines in the darkness which neither understands nor overcomes it. The idea of darkness has traditionally been tied to the power of evil (Satan was known as "The Prince of Darkness"). The New Testament is saturated with the idea that the world is not in God's control at all – it is in the control of evil forces. Christ shines as a light in the world of darkness, his followers are called to be lights in the world and not to let their lights be hidden. Nowhere is the power of evil over the world more clearly depicted than in the story of the temptation of Jesus in the wilderness:

> Then the Devil took him up and showed him in a second all the kingdoms of the world. "I will give you all this power and all this wealth," the Devil told him. "It has all been handed over to me, and I can give it to anyone I choose. All this will be yours, then, if you worship me."

(Luke 4:5-7, Good News Bible)

This is a very significant passage (to which we shall return in chapter 15). The import is clear, that the forces of evil have power over all the kingdoms of the world and can use this power in any way they choose. It is not obvious who has "handed over" this power. There are two alternatives – either God or human beings. The passage is ambiguous. The Book of Job makes clear that the Devil only has power if God permits this and the passage could imply that the power has been given by God. Perhaps it would be more accurate to see God as allowing human beings to hand over control of themselves and of their world to the forces of chaos, evil and darkness – thereby placing themselves in bondage to these forces. God can still be held to be totally omnipotent in that he *could* overthrow the power of the forces of evil, but he could only do this at the price of overthrowing the established order with all the possibilities it contains.

In chapter 14 we shall return to what it means to talk about the Devil, for now the important point is to recognize that the New Testament does not picture God as being in control of the world. The Gospels do not give the picture of an omnipotent God who can do anything he wills. The powers of the forces of light are distinctly limited. Jesus coming into the world is, indeed, seen as the entry of light into a world which is in the grip of evil forces. Jesus' arrival is like a candle, albeit one that cannot and will not ever be put out. It only needs one candle to make an enormous difference in a sea of darkness and so Jesus was decisive in rolling back the forces of evil. His disciples draw strength from him and their own lights, reflecting his, shine out in the encircling gloom. Other disciples take this light and gradually and with enormous difficulty and at great cost try to reduce the power of evil. So the process continues down the centuries.

Only at the most enormous cost and with the greatest difficulty can the control exercised by the forces of pride, of selfishness and of greed be overcome. A world plunged in darkness can be redeemed by the power of light and love but it is not easy. God's intervention in Jesus is decisive but it is not final. The only real power God has is the guarantee that he provides that anyone who anchors him or herself wholly on him will not be overcome by the forces of darkness. This is expressed by St Paul saying:

I am certain that nothing can separate us from his love; neither death nor life, neither angels nor other heavenly rulers or powers, neither the present nor the future, neither the world above nor the world below – there is nothing in all creation that will ever be able to separate us from the love of God which is ours through Christ Jesus our Lord.

(Romans 8:38–9)

"Nothing can separate us from the love of God which is in Christ Jesus" – the one thing that the individual can be sure of is that, no matter what the opposition of the forces of darkness, if he or she will genuinely anchor him or herself wholly on God, nothing will be able to break this tie. This, however, does not guarantee exemption from earthly suffering. Pain, misunderstandings, opposition, rejection, unpopularity, prison and even death in some countries will be the expected lot for anyone following this path. Trusting in God is in no way an exemption from these hardships. The only thing that God can give is the power to withstand them and to cope.

This position has been accepted by Christians throughout the centuries, yet in spite of this theologians and philosophers have insisted on talking of God's omnipotent power. Naturally such talk leads people to ask why God does not do away with evil. If God's power in the world is unlimited, it is an entirely reasonable question. Only when it is recognized that God's power is very limited indeed does his lack of activity to overcome evil by direct action make sense.

Muslims believe that everything happens by God's will. "It is the will of Allah" is the cornerstone phrase of their faith. Nothing can happen except by God's will. Many Christians take a similar position.

In a little village near where I live in the depths of rural England, a young couple had their five-year-old son killed by falling into a river. They were Christians and were finally comforted by an evangelical preacher who explained to them that the death of their son was God's will and that their son had been taken to be with God. I believe this view to be profoundly and radically wrong.

Similarly I believe the Muslim insistence on the dominance of the "will of Allah" is gravely mistaken.

Everything that happens does not happen by God's will. This view takes the idea of God's omnipotence and providence far too literally. It emphasizes God's providential care at the price of human dignity and human freedom. A God who could seriously wish to kill a five-year-old child is not a God worth worshipping. A God who can control everything that happens and who allows so much suffering in the world is a malevolent God.

The following anonymous sixteenth-century poem expresses God's providential control in the world beautifully – but its beauty does not prevent it from being theologically mistaken:

> Man's life is laid in the loom of time
> To a pattern he does not see,
> while the weavers work and the shuttles fly
> till the dawn of eternity.
> Some shuttles are filled with silver threads
> and some with threads of gold,
> While often but the darker hues
> are all that they may hold.
> But the weaver watches with skilful eye
> Each shuttle fly to and fro,
> And sees the pattern so deftly wrought
> as the loom moves sure and slow.
> God surely planned the pattern
> each thread the dark and fair,
> is chosen by his master's skill
> and placed in the web with care.
> He only knows its beauty
> And guides the shuttles which hold,
> the threads so unattractive
> As well as the threads of gold.
> Not till each loom is silent

and the shuttles cease to fly,
Shall God reveal the pattern
and explain the reason why
the dark threads were as needful
in the weaver's skilful hand,
as the threads of gold and silver
for the pattern which he planned.

To hold that God plans each thread of our lives with care makes him into an obscene God, not a loving God. God does not want suffering, he does not will evil, he does not use suffering as a means to some wider end. Jesus fought against evils, he cried when Lazarus died. Compassion and God's tender care was central to his message.

Jesus' power was very limited in comparison with those of the forces ranged against him. His power was shown in weakness, not in omnipotent strength. It was a power that came from refusing to retaliate against those who mocked and derided him, against those who spat on him and crucified him. It was the power of gentleness and love which depends on a free response from individual human beings. In the end this can overcome all enemies, but at tremendous cost. It was a power that called his disciples to take nothing with them when they went on the road and to rely on hospitality wherever they went; that called people to turn the other cheek, to travel the extra mile; that called the rich to abandon their reliance on their wealth; that called people to leave the dead to bury their own dead; to sell everything to gain the treasure of great price and that demanded that everything in life should be put in second place to the call and faith placed in God alone.

This faith was not, however, a faith that would keep his followers immune from harm. Stephen was stoned to death, Paul was continually persecuted, Peter crucified upside down, tens of thousands of Christians were sent to the lions or used as human torches by Nero and subsequent Roman emperors. Even today Christians are persecuted – six Jesuits were murdered in Chile in 1989; the Anglican

Archbishop of Uganda was tortured and put to death; Martin Luther King was assassinated and so the story continues throughout the world. Following Jesus was never going to be a pleasant business. It would set members of families against each other, it would involve great sacrifice and suffering and constant opposition. Christianity might be seen as involving, in Hamlet's ringing phrase: "to take arms against a sea of troubles and by opposing them – To die? – to sleep? . . . perchance to dream . . .". Individuals are called to take a personal stand against a sea of darkness and, in opposing these forces, to suffer and be persecuted. Unlike Hamlet, however, they can know that God provides a sure and certain anchor, death and dreams hold no fears.

Jesus' power did not prevail against the will of those who set themselves against him. It was a power of persuasion and, even when miracles were performed, they depended on faith. Jesus could not perform miracles where there was little faith and he could do nothing to help himself.

It seems strange that given the Gospel pictures and the extraordinary nature of Jesus' power, the idea should have grown that God is omnipotent in the world, a God of power and might. Jesus always said his kingdom was not of this world and the same applies to his power. If we measure God by worldly standards of power, then he is very far from omnipotent.

If we accept the "given" with which this second part of the book commenced – that God can correctly be described as personal, loving and Almighty, as three persons in one, and who can be conceived as the creator and sustainer of the universe who interacts with his creation and who calls human beings to respond to him in love both for himself and for each other – then how do we reconcile the apparent awesome power possessed by this God with the apparent impotence of God to act in the world implied by the Gospels? There are various alternatives:

1. To regard God as limited by the power of an equal and opposite force to him. On this view, there are two Gods – one good and

one evil. These two forces are at war and the outcome is uncertain.
This type of cosmic dualism has always been rejected by traditional
Christianity as God is no longer the sole creator and sustainer of
the universe and I have argued against it on p.69.

2. The second position is much more persuasive, although it has
not been actively supported by Christian theologians. Plato
maintained that his God, the Demiurge, fashioned the universe out
of chaotic matter which he did not create. Just as a potter moulds
but does not create the clay, so God moulded the raw matter of
the universe. If a similar approach is taken, the Christian God could
rightly be described as creator because he moulded and fashioned
raw, chaotic matter – he brought order out of chaos. There are two
accounts of the creation of the world in the book of Genesis and
they are very different. Both, however, can be regarded as supporting
this view. For instance:

> In the beginning, when God created the universe, the earth was
> formless and desolate. The raging ocean that covered everything
> was engulfed in total darkness and the power of God was moving
> over the water. Then God commanded, "Let there be light . . ."
>
> (Genesis 1:1–3)

> When the Lord God made the universe, there were no plants
> on the earth and no seeds had sprouted, because he had not sent
> any rain, and there was no-one to cultivate the land, but water
> would come up from beneath the surface and water the ground.
> Then the Lord God took some soil from the ground and formed
> a man out of it; he breathed life-giving breath into his nostrils
> and the man began to live.
>
> (Genesis 2:4b–7)

In the first account, the "formless and desolate" earth could well
resemble the primeval chaos. In the second account, the earth clearly

existed and was awaiting plants and animals. In neither account is there any suggestion of creation out of nothing.

If, therefore, raw matter is considered to exist independent of God, then God could, through his action, be seen to be bringing order out of chaos. The raw matter continuously resists his will and seeks to descend once more into chaos. This is an attractive account, and intellectually it has a great deal to commend it. However, the independence of matter from God is a real limitation and is not something that many theologians would be willing to accept – although, of course, this does not prove it to be false.

3. God created the universe in such a way that, necessarily, his power over it is limited. This seems much the most persuasive approach. God created the universe as it is and built into this universe are certain constraints on God's freedom of action – restraints that cannot be removed without destroying the universe as it is. This sounds fine, but the problem comes with the word "necessarily". *Why* is God's power *necessarily* limited? Why could God not have created an identical universe save that he had more power?

To answer this question it is necessary to understand how finely the universe is balanced. We now know a great deal about the development of the universe from the initial "Big Bang". At the Big Bang, matter flew apart at phenomenal speed. Ever since, suns, planets and interstellar matter have been coalescing and going further and further apart from the force of the initial explosion. However, this force is counteracted by the force of gravity and we know that the various forces are incredibly finely balanced. If the amount of matter involved in the initial explosion had been slightly greater then the force of gravity would have caused the universe to collapse in on itself, while if the amount of matter had been less then the universe would have flown apart so quickly that stars would not have formed (see p.16). The forces holding the universe together are thus in unbelievably fine equilibrium (making, incidentally, the idea of chance being solely responsible for the existence of the universe rather less credible).

Similarly the conditions for life as we know it on planet Earth are very finely balanced. We know this all too clearly now as we begin to see the effects which our interference with the balance causes. The ozone layer is depleted by our use of CFC gases, the increase of carbon dioxide emissions threatens us with the greenhouse effect and pollution is destroying many of our seas. The whole of creation is finely tuned, it simply is not possible to alter one aspect of the planet without affecting others.

The third of the above alternatives appears the most likely as well as being most in line with the mainstream Christian tradition, even though it does not fully answer the atheist's challenge as to why God could not have created a universe with different physical laws. As we saw in the first part of this book, however, there may be no adequate answer to this challenge – which is one reason why faith and reason may be in tension. If God indeed exists (as is assumed in chapter 7) and if God created the universe in order to provide the conditions for free human beings to emerge and to choose for or against the possibility of fellowship with him, then the number of available options for God must have been strictly limited. The world contains incredible beauty from the cosmological to the microscopic level, it obeys standard laws which operate over vast distances, and human beings are able to improve the world in which they live. They can inflict great harm on each other and on their environment, but there is also the opportunity for great virtue, courage and fortitude. Above all, the conditions are ideally suited for the emergence of free, rational human beings who are capable of love. If free, rational beings are indeed a central part of God's plan, then God's remaining options would have been very limited indeed. In particular, God would not be able to intervene frequently without destroying the structure of the universe. Any intervention has widespread effects – it is not limited to the event itself. In the succeeding chapter in which we examine what it means to say that

God acts in the world we will have to elaborate further on this.

To call God Almighty, therefore, is to recognize the ultimate dependence of the universe and all things within it on God. It is to recognize God's creative and sustaining power. However it specifically does not mean that God has total power to do anything he wishes. God is limited by the universe he has chosen to create. It presumably would be logically possible for him to bring this universe and its structures to an end, but as long as the universe continues his power to act will be much restricted by his free decision to limit himself. This limitation does not, however, lessen God in any significant way. It is rather a recognition of God's wish to create a universe in which human beings can be brought into a loving relationship with him. God will still be able to act in the world – although the scope for this action will be limited. We must now turn to examine what possibilites for action are available to God.

To summarize, the believer can make the following statements which could express his or her position so far:

i) I accept the existence of a creator God as previously defined.

ii) I make a supreme value judgement by which I hold that the ultimate purpose and meaning for human existence is to be found only in fellowship with and love of God and living out this love in a life of self-giving love to those around us. For this reason I call God good as God is the ultimate source of everything I value most highly. Evil represents anything that makes it more difficult for individuals to achieve this purpose.

iii) I accept that God is Almighty, but by this I do not mean that God is able to exercise total power over the forces of evil in the world. God's power is shown in weakness. Nothing can separate me from God's love and because of this God can help me to overcome evil even though this may lead to suffering.

ELEVEN

Can God Act in the World?

> My God, my God, why have you abandoned me?
> I have cried desperately for help,
> but still it does not come.
> "You relied on the Lord," they say.
> "Why doesn't he save you?"
>
> Psalm 22:1, 8

If God is able to act in the world to prevent or overcome evil and yet fails to do so, then it can be argued that God is morally culpable and directly to blame for much of the world's sufferings – which God could alleviate if he chose to do so. Of all the charges made against God, this is one of the most powerful. The attack has been put persuasively by two modern Philosophers of Religion – Brian Hebblethwaite of Cambridge and Maurice Wiles of Oxford:

> If it really is God's way to intervene miraculously to bring about his purposes . . . then why does he not do so more often and to greater effect?
>
> (Hebblethwaite, *Divine Action*, 1976)

If the direct action of God, independent of secondary causation, is to be an intelligible concept, then it would appear to have been sparingly and strangely used. Miracles must by definition be relatively infrequent or . . . ordered life as we know it would be an impossibility. Yet even so it would seem strange that no miraculous intervention prevented Auschwitz or Hiroshima, whilst the purposes apparently forwarded by some of the miracles acclaimed in traditional Christian faith seem trivial by comparison . . .

("God's action in the world", SCM, p.66)

These are persuasive and important points. If God can really intervene in the world and, for instance, bring about miraculous cures in Lourdes or arrange for Jesus or the Virgin Mary to appear to young girls, if believers consider that God listens to their petitions and acts in response to them, then why does God not similarly act to alleviate the terrible suffering in Auschwitz, in Stalin's death camps; the pain suffered by victims of cancer or the effects of earthquakes or tidal waves? Once it is accepted that it is possible for God to act, God's failure to act more comprehensively creates a real problem for believers.

Maurice Wiles, in reflecting on this, comes to the conclusion that God should be denied the freedom to act in the world. In other words we should reject the idea of an intervening God. Other philosophers such as Gareth Moore O.P. take a similar line when they say that no event can be correctly described by saying "God did it" ("Believing in God – A Philosophic Essay").

Wiles does not, however, reject belief in God. He maintains that God does act, but only by means of a single creative act. In his single creative act, God brings the world into existence, sustains it and supports its unfolding. Everything can be seen to be part of the one act of God. However, if everything is part of God's one single act, it is wrong to think of particular events being brought about by God in a way that others are not. A God who intervenes selectively would not be worthy of worship because of his failure to act on a wider scale.

To deny to God the "freedom to act without causal restrain in the world" may not in fact be to depersonalize him but be rather a corollary of the kind of world God has in fact chosen to create.

(p.80)

Wiles' restriction on God also applies to God's action in Christ. It will not do, he considers, to restrict God to two acts – namely the incarnation and resurrection. As Leslie Houlden says:

> The isolation of incarnation and resurrection as prime and crucial instances of direct divine action, while it may seem a concession to modernity, effectively falsifies the role they formally played. Once peaks in a landscape full of hills, all seen as such instances, they now stand out like naked pillars of rock in a plain.
>
> (Review of W. J. Abraham's "Divine Revelation and the Limits of Historical Criticism" in JTS XXXIV, April 1983, p.378)

Wiles therefore maintains that an alternative way must be found to embody the convictions in the doctrines of the incarnation and resurrection which do not involve any breach in the structure of the known world. Wiles maintains that the incarnation, instead of being seen as an action by God, should instead be thought of in terms of the perfection of human response to God. The full humanity of Jesus has always been a central part of Christian teaching and this would include "the same human freedom which is constitutive of our existence as persons" (p.87). Jesus freely and fully responded totally to God's grace and in so doing incarnated God in the world. Wiles claims support from Hans Küng for this type of approach when Küng says:

> . . . the raising of Jesus is not a miracle violating the laws of nature . . . not a supernatural intervention which can be located and dated in space and time.
>
> (*On Being a Christian*, Collins, p.349)

and Wiles concludes that:

> It seems to me no clearer theologically than historically that this final coping-stone, faith in the vindication of Jesus and the

conviction that Jesus lives in the presence of God, could only have derived from some special action of God in the form of supernaturally given appearances of Jesus.

(p.92)

If Wiles' view is accepted, it has profound consequences. In particular, any idea of miracles as direct actions by God would have to be abandoned. Belief in petitionary prayer, seen as the believer asking God to do things in the world with the expectation that there is at least the possibility of God responding to this prayer and bringing about states of affairs that would not have occurred were it not for the prayer, would have to be rejected. The status of the incarnate Christ would also be subtly changed into a fully human figure who perfectly responded to God's call. These are substantial alterations to traditional Christian doctrine.

The believer is apparently faced with a dilemma. Either to accept Wiles' view and to abandon belief in miracles and petitionary prayer as traditionally understood or else to affirm the possibility of selective action but then have to accept that God's chosen actions seem to be arbitrary and that God must be held morally responsible for failing to reduce the amount of evil in the world by direct action.

It is not easy explaining why prayers are not answered; why an innocent child who is prayed for by his devout parents and friends still dies; why prayers for peace seem to be ignored; and how to justify God's apparently arbitrary action. Wiles' refusal to countenance selective action by God dissolves these problems and is very attractive indeed – although the price paid is considerable.

I want to maintain that Maurice Wiles is wrong and that it is possible to understand selective action by God in a way that makes sense to the believer and accounts for the facts. Wiles is right to say that the sort of world God creates imposes limitations on God, but he has set the limits far too wide and has thereby effectively made God impotent.

The explanation I want to suggest follows on from the last chapter in which God's almighty power in the world is held to be restricted. However there is a very significant difference between saying that God's action is restricted and maintaining, as Wiles does, that God cannot act at all. If the aim of the whole of creation is to creat free, rational beings intended for fellowship with God, then the freedom of these individuals is vital. Any action by God must, therefore, not interfere with this freedom.

God could act in the world in a way which would make his presence completely obvious. One could imagine Star Wars lights over New York and lightning bolts striking offending people or objects. Such obvious action would inspire awe, wonder and terror. There would be no doubting the obedience of most people as the sanction of the power-figure-in-the-sky would be immediate and effective. Disobedience would be punished and obedience would be rewarded. One would be in the world of George Orwell's *1984*. Just as Big Brother was held to watch everything, so the C.I.A., the Celestial Intelligence Agency, would be known to watch the believer's every move.

In the temptations in the wilderness, the Devil offers Jesus the possibility of this type of approach. It is interesting and highly significant that nowhere in the Gospels is Jesus or God held to have complete power in the world. It is, as we saw in the previous chapter, the Devil in the wilderness who offers Jesus this power, almost as a derivative of his own power, again emphasizing that the real and effective power in the world is the power of evil, not of God. Certainly Jesus is held to have had some power. Jesus could have thrown himself down from the Temple in Jerusalem in full view of thousands of Jews and Romans. Angels would then have scooped him up and everyone would immediately have believed in him. The key point is, however, that this was a temptation. If Jesus had succumbed to this temptation it would have totally undermined his purposes. The reason is simple – God's highest priority is not to bring people to obedience, but to love. Obedience is easily organized; provided the power is great enough and the sanctions heavy enough, individuals can be coerced into obedience (George Orwell's book *1984* is a good illustration of this). In fact, freedom is not even necessary for obedience. Human beings could have been created like robots so that they would always do exactly what their creator wished. It is much easier to create robots than to create free human beings.

God's purpose is, however, to create free human beings who can choose what to make of themselves. This is the terrifying responsibility that human beings have. We actually have the ability to decide what sort of people to become. We can choose to make ourselves into people who can love, people who show gentleness, compassion and concern for others, who are willing to put themselves in second place to the needs of others and the commands of God or we can choose to follow our own path and our own inclinations. However, if we are really to be able to exercise this choice, then this imposes much greater limits on God's ability to act. An example will illustrate the problem.

Imagine a young and beautiful coal miner's daughter living in a remote pit village in a central European kingdom. Imagine further that the King had once seen this girl when he was out hunting and fell totally in love with her. He thought about her constantly and loved her passionately. He wished to woo her and to bring her to love him – yet how should he proceed? If he were to ride to the village with all his retainers, the girl would be terrified. If he stepped down and spoke to her in his magnificent robes, she would quake with terror. If he said that he loved her it simply would not make sense. She would be so full of fear, so awe-struck, so intimidated that she would not be able to respond. Her fear would lead her to go along with whatever the King wished, but then she would not love him. The problem was that the King did not want to seduce her, he did not want to command her obedience, to intimidate her or make her his servant – he loved her and he wanted her to love him. Nothing else would do.

If the King persisted in his love, he really only has one alternative.

Of course his courtiers are likely to say that he is mad – why, after all, should the King bother with a poor, insignificant peasant girl? If he wanted her, he has but to command and she has no choice but to obey. If the King insisted on giving her a choice, she is still certain to do as he wishes because she could not refuse him anything. The King sees, however, that the courtiers have misunderstood. They do not understand love. If the King truly loved the young girl, then he would never intimidate or frighten her. He would not be interested in a relationship with her that is built on fear. Only one thing is good enough – and that is a relationship of love.

The King, therefore, has no alternative. He must go to the young girl in disguise. Not dressed in his fine robes but rather in old clothes, the clothes of a wandering tradesman perhaps. He must hope that, when she sees him and gets to know him, she will fall in love with him. If she does, her love will then be free. She will love him for himself and not for any ulterior motive. She will not think of his money, or his power, of the comforts she could enjoy nor will she be full of fear of the consequences of not loving. She will love him for himself alone. There are, of course, risks. The young girl may not like the King. She may reject him. This, however, is the risk that love runs. It can never be forced and it must risk rejection and disappointment.

The parallel, of course, is with God. If God appeared on earth as he is, everyone would be terror-struck. Immediate obedience would be automatic. The creator of the universe disclosing himself as he is, would be more than man could cope with. The Jews recognized that no man could see God and live – he had to hide himself.

God, therefore, has to hide his actions. These actions cannot be obvious if human freedom is to be respected. Even the biggest intervention of all, the sending of Jesus, had to be undertaken in a way that would preserve human freedom and allow the possibility of love. By sending Jesus in the form of a working tradesman, as an ordinary human being, the Godhead is effectively disguised. No proofs were possible as to who he was without taking away freedom. Jesus himself refused proofs of who he was. He rejected performing miracles in order to secure belief – indeed he often told those he healed not to tell anyone that the healing had taken place. He wanted people to recognize who he was, what he stood for without any magic tricks to act as a guarantee. David Hume was radically wrong when he maintained that miracles act as a foundation for faith – they never have and have never been intended to fulfil this function.

When Jesus stood before Pilate, he was asked, "What is truth?" Pilate sought truth that could be proved, truth that was objective. Yet no proof would be possible that would not take away freedom – that was what the temptation in the wilderness was all about. If Pilate could not recognize that Jesus was the Truth when Jesus was standing in front of him, there was nothing more to be said. Faith is always based on ambiguity and never on certainty. There is no proof available that God exists or that Jesus was God incarnate – it is a step of trust, requiring a personal decision or, as we saw in chapter 9, an absolute value judgement. When Jesus asked Peter, "Who do you say that I am?", he was asking Peter to make a stand, to declare himself. When John the Baptist's disciples came to Jesus from John who was in prison, asking whether he was the Messiah or whether John should be looking for another, Jesus did not reply directly – instead he told the disciples to go to John, to report on what they had seen and to let John make up his own mind.

If faith is to be preserved, if love is to be possible, if the ambiguity of God's actions is to be maintained then they must be hidden and less than obvious. It follows, therefore, that any action by God cannot be readily identified. If people pray for peace in Northern Ireland and it is simply brought about by divine fiat, then human freedom would be destroyed. If a child has cancer and is simply cured by a miracle, then the ambiguity of faith would be denied.

God's ability to act is, however, even more limited than this. To illustrate the next restriction, it may be helpful to digress into the world of science fiction. Isaac Asimov was, arguably, the greatest science fiction writer of all time. He has written a series of five books which make up the "Foundation" series. The books are set thousands of years in the future. A galactic empire has been established under which planets from all over the galaxy, all of which are peopled with human beings and complex civilizations, are governed from the imperial capital, the world of Trantor. The Empire is at its height and its ubiquitous power seems undoubted. One man, however, does doubt the Empire's power and sees the cracks beneath the glittering facade. This man is a mathematician called Hari Seldon who develops a new science called "Psychohistory". This combines psychology and prediction of the future based on the predictability of human behaviour. By the advanced mathematics that are then available and detailed statistical analysis, Hari Seldon realizes that it is possible to predict the future intentions and actions of huge groups of people. Whereas the actions of individuals are unpredictable, the actions of hundreds of millions can be predicted.

Seldon realizes that the galactic Empire is beginning to collapse, although there will be no apparent evidence of this collapse for hundreds of years. He knows that the Empire will sink into the dark ages with individual planetary groups at war with each other (there could be parallels with the break-up of the Russian Empire and the nationalist tendencies that have emerged in the different republics). Nothing can prevent the collapse of the galactic Empire, but something can be done to lessen the period of chaos before the next Empire comes into being.

Hari Seldon arranges to establish two Foundations, one at each end of the galaxy. The first Foundation is science-based. Seldon persuades the Emperor to allow him to collect together on a small and insignificant planet some of the finest minds in the galaxy whose ostensible purpose is to prepare a galactic encyclopaedia which would maintain and preserve all the knowledge in the galaxy. The scientists duly assemble on the little world of Terminus, a world with few natural resources at the very edge of the galaxy. As the Empire gradually dies, the science-based world of Terminus is forced to adapt, to develop new technologies and to cope with the political changes that the dying Empire causes. Various crises emerge and although Hari Seldon has died, his psychohistory enabled him to predict these crises and also the likelihood of them being successfully overcome.

In due course, it emerges that the second of the two Foundations is radically different from the first. It is based on mental power rather than physical power. It consists of psychohistorians who have developed their mental powers and mathematical models of human behaviour to extraordinary degrees. They are few in number, but their task is to guide the development of Terminus (the centre of the First Foundation) to produce a new and better galactic Empire after the collapse of the first.

The story unfolds over the centuries. The First Foundation faces numerous crises which it surmounts with varying degrees of ease. At each stage it becomes clear that Hari Seldon had predicted the crisis and predicted how it would be overcome. Inevitably, however, events begin to deviate from Seldon's original plan and this is where the psychohistorians of the Second Foundation come in – making very small mental adjustments in the behaviour of individual human beings to keep the plan on track. The psychohistorians, however, have to exercise great care to remain unknown and to ensure that the effects that their actions will have are wholly predictable. Tiny actions can and do reverberate down the centuries. A seemingly insignificant action can have monumental effects.

The same, I want to argue, applies in the case of God's interventions in the world. Any intervention by God has enormous effects and, in particular, human freedom is likely to be massively affected. God has to restrict his actions, just like the psychohistorians of Asimov's science fiction have to restrict theirs.

It simply is not possible for human beings to be aware of the consequences of actions. One tiny action can have enormous and unpredictable effects. God would know the effects that interventions could have and, therefore, has to restrict his actions to those which owuld either have minimal effects or those whose effects would not unduly interfere with human freedom. God's biggest action, which undoubtedly had enormous effects, of sending his son to the world was nevertheless done in such a way as to maximize human freedom.

To expect God, therefore, just to intervene to cope with crises in the world is incredibly naïve. It cannot work like that, any actions by God will be sparingly and occasionally used. No other choice is possible if the radical freedom of creation is to be maintained.

Keith Ward has gone some way towards recognizing this position. In his book *Divine Action* (HarperCollinsFlame, 1990), he discusses the problem of petitionary prayer. Ward accepts the existence of the traditional idea of God although he appears to work with a temporal rather than a timeless God. He considers the question of whether God would really allow himself to be influenced by human requests. On the face of it, it would be irrational for God to be influenced by any petitionary prayers – God, after all, knows better than any human being what it is best to do. He knows what we want before we ask and since he will do what is best whether or not we pray our requests seem irrelevant.

Ward argues that it is not true to say that God always does what is best. This is because there is often no single "best" actions. As Ward says:

> God always has options for action, options limited by many constraints of structure and human response. In such a system, God may well choose one option – indeed, an option may become open to him within the constraints of the system – precisely because a creature who loves God desires it and asks God for it.
>
> (p.159)

Ward sees the individual, in prayer, opening him- or herself to the divine will, but also seeking to influence this will. God cannot be manipulated by human beings, but if the divine plan is to a large extent open, God may realize a certain state of affairs just because it has been requested. The making of the request is an additional state of affairs which God will take into account. Ward, therefore, actually sees God modifying his plans for the world to take account of human requests.

Is it possible that God should have his mind changed by petitionary prayer? Ward answers as follows:

> As God may justly leave many outcomes to free human choice, and not determine them himself, so he may permit some outcomes that he would otherwise determine himself to be modified and directed by human choices, in the form of requests made to him in the context of worship. Prayer is then seen as an extension of human freedom. We are not only free to perform certain acts, thus bringing about states of affairs by our choice, but we are also free to ask God to bring about some states of affairs, and thus bring them about by our requests.
>
> (pp.160–1)

This is an important and radical view which dramatically increases our ideas about the area of human freedom. Not only are human beings free, but we can use our freedom to influence God. We cannot, of course, control God, but by living in relationship with God – a genuine personal relationship – the possibility is open for God to be influenced by our requests. This is a move that few theologians or philosophers of religion have been willing to make, partly because they have worked with the timeless and totally unchanging God of Aquinas who cannot be changed by human requests. As Aquinas puts it:

> We do not pray in order to change the decree of divine providence, rather we pray in order to acquire by petitionary prayer what God has determined would be obtained by our prayers.
>
> (ST, 2a, 2ae, 83)

This seems to involve a high degree of predestination and Ward moves outside the seeming straitjacket imposed by the Thomist God.

Ward's approach is helpful and my main reservation is that he overestimates God's power and the efficacy of God's divine plan. As I have tried to argue, I believe that the world is much more outside God's control than Ward seems to imply. However, given that God may be able to act in some circumstances in the world, then Ward seems to me to be right in making room for the possibility of God being influenced in his actions by human requests.

Human beings must also have the ability to prevent God's actions, to shut God out. Basinger ("Why petition an Omnipotent, Omniscient and wholly good God?", Religious Studies, 19) asks:

> If we assume that God simply imposes his will on free moral agents, is it possible to envision many situations in which God might desire to intervene . . . in the life of an individual but not be able to do so unless personally requested?

This, then is another limitation on God's freedom to act. God does not coerce, God rather lures human beings. Coercion would take away freedom while God is concerned to draw people to him freely so that they can respond in love. It follows that people must be able to shut themselves off from God, to prevent God acting through them. As Basinger puts it:

> . . . such a God would in general need to limit himself to the continual offering of general guidance and the occasional offering of specific guidance or direct intervention.

God could act to help individuals to be clear on his will so that they could follow him, but only if they had opened themselves to his guidance first of all. Human response to God is, therefore, of tremendous importance – it is a necessary condition for God being able to act at all, just as faith was a necessary condition for Jesus being able to act.

To summarize, then, I have maintained that God can act selectively in the world and that he is not the impotent deity that Wiles claims. However, his ability to act is much more limited than many assume. The limitations are not due to divine whim, but to three main factors:

1. As we saw in the last chapter, God is not omnipotent in the world. His freedom of action is greatly proscribed as he is operating in a world that is largely outside of his control.

2. In addition, if the possibility of faith and love is to be retained, any action by God needs to be ambiguous – it must be capable of being interpreted in more than one way.

3. Since any action has enormous effects, God can only act in those cases where his action would have minimal long-term effects or where it would not interfere with human freedom. He can act to lure people to him, but not to compel them to his service.

In this account, room is available for direct divine action either directly or through people, but this action is going to be sparingly used. It will only occur where it is necessary to foster faith, to strengthen the flickering lights in the world. He loved us so that he gave us freedom to choose to love him in return, or to turn away. In such a world, the consequences of human actions are the responsibility of humanity – the world is largely outside God's control and so the power of God to act is correspondingly restricted.

We can, therefore, add one further statement to those that a believer can make in relation to the problem of evil. The full set so far is as follows:

i) I accept the existence of a creator God as previously defined.

ii) I make a supreme value judgement by which I hold that the ultimate purpose and meaning for human existence is to be found only in fellowship with and love of God and living out this love in a life of self-giving love to those around us. For this reason I call God good as God is the ultimate source of everything I value most highly. Evil represents anything that makes it more difficult for individuals to achieve this purpose.

iii) I accept that God is Almighty, but by this I do not mean that God is able to exercise total power over the forces of evil in the world (chapter 10). God's power is shown in weakness. Nothing can separate me from God's love and because of this God can help me to overcome evil even though this may lead to suffering.

iv) I believe that God can act in the world in response to the prayers of believers. God cannot, however, be controlled but he can and does answer prayers. However, such actions by God are going to be rare and will be sparingly used. We cannot see the possible effects of divine interventions and, in placing our petitions before God, must nevertheless accept that his will should be done as only he can see the implications of any possible action. Prayer therefore involves trust.

TWELVE

Animal Suffering and Physical Evil

> I am God, your God . . .
> all the animals of the forest are mine,
> and the cattle on thousands of hills,
> All the wild birds are mine,
> and all living things in the fields.
>
> (Psalm 50:7, 9–10)

Darwin showed that the survival of the fittest is the key mechanism which causes evolutionary changes and maintains and improves the quality of the gene pool. On this model, human beings can seem of no importance and countless millions of types of animals appear to be no more than means to some blind end. Tennyson portrayed the problem this way in his poem "Ulysses" in 1850:

> Are God and Nature then at strife,
> That Nature lends such evil dreams?
> So careful of the type she seems,
> So careless of the single life.
>
> "So careful of the type?" but no,
> From scarped cliff and quarried stone
> She cries, "A thousand types are gone:
> I care for nothing, all shall go."
>
> Man, her last work, who seem'd so fair
> Such splendid purpose in his eyes
> Who roll'd the psalm to wintry skies
> Who built him fanes of fruitless prayer

Animal Suffering and Physical Evil

Who trusted God was love indeed
  And love creation's final law –
  Tho' Nature, red in tooth and claw
With ravine shrieked against his creed

Who lov'd, who suffered countless ills
  Who battled for the True, the Just
  Be blown about the desert dust
Or seal'd within the iron hills?

(From Sections LV and LVI)

Could not God have created a universe in which the developing world could have been brought about with less extreme pain and suffering, where all animals only ate grass and did not prey on each other?

Clearly such a world would be radically different from this one. All animals would grow old and die of natural causes. The world would either become quickly overpopulated or else the reproductive rate would have to be drastically reduced. Many species would die of starvation as the plant resources on which they fed were used up by other animals. The whole idea of evolution would have to be abandoned as the "survival of the fittest" is the most effective tool to ensure evolutionary quality. In the absence of this mechanism, the weak and maimed animals would survive and their genes would be passed on into the gene pool thus weakening it still further.

The alternative to evolution is not a pleasant pastoral scene but rather a decadent world. When progress stops then the gene pool rapidly becomes impoverished. The struggle to survive is essential not just in the animal but also in the human world. The fact that existence is a struggle and that it is difficult is the factor that pushes plants, animals and humans on to new heights of development and achievement. It maintains varying species in balance with each other and ensures adaptation can take place to meet varying physical and environmental conditions. Even in the human sphere, the struggle against adversity may well be a necessary condition for spiritual development. Christian saints have generally emerged from harsh conditions and under severe testing. Where there is no challenge there is likely to be little faith.

We know that conditions on earth have varied considerably over billions of years. The ice age first advanced and then receded and brought enormous changes in climate. Plants and animals adapted to these changes. Evolution enabled the life of the world to be self-sustaining, to have tremendous diversity with different species adapted to different conditions, all the time maintaining a perfect balance. Dinosaurs probably died out because of changed conditions, but other species took over. The richness of our animal and plant heritage is due to the high rate of fecundity, the high rate of mortality and the adaptability of animal species.

James Lovelock in his book *Gaia – the practical science of planetary medicine* (Gaia Books, 1991), argues that the earth is an inter-dependent whole. Human beings are a part of this whole and exist only because the very delicate balance that permits life is maintained. If we abuse this balance the planet as a whole will no longer accept human life. Instead of seeing human beings as masters of our environment, Lovelock maintains that we should see ourselves as part of the environment, part of a whole which is "Gaia" representing the whole earth system.

To reject evolution, therefore, is not to reject a harsh way of creating a world in favour of a gentler one. It is to reject the best and most effective way of creating a world of great beauty, richness, diversity and adaptability which has within it the possibility of love and the higher virtues.

Few theologians have taken animal suffering at all seriously or, indeed, the clear scientific evidence of man's position in the world. Animals and the whole environment have generally been regarded as existing for the benefit of man and it is only recently that people have woken up to the fact that they have a responsibility for the earth and the animals and plants it contains. Previously the earth and its contents were seen to be resources to be exploited for the good of human beings. The Genesis stories of the creation contain two apparently conflicting approaches to man's role in relation to the rest of creation. In the first chapter it says:

> God blessed them, saying to them, "Be fruitful, multiply, fill the earth and conquer it. Be masters of the fish of the deep, the birds of heaven and all living animals on the earth."
>
> (Genesis 1:28–9, Jerusalem Bible)

The words "conquer" and "Be masters" clearly indicate an attitude of supremacy. The earth is there to be used for the needs of human beings. However the story in the second chapter of Genesis gives a different picture:

> Yahweh planted a garden in Eden which is in the east and there he put the man he had fashioned . . . Yahweh took the man and settled him in the garden of Eden to cultivate and take care of it.
>
> (Genesis 2:8,15, Jerusalem Bible)

Here we have a radically altered impression. To "cultivate and take care of" implies that human beings are part of the earth with responsibility for it. God created human beings as part of the environment, not exploiters of it. The second chapter of Genesis even has God creating man from the dust of the earth:

> Then the Lord God took some soil from the ground and formed a man out of it; he breathed life-giving breath into his nostrils.
>
> (Genesis 2:7, Good News Bible)

The tendency has been to emphasize the first of the two Genesis accounts at the expense of the second. Christian leaders have paid lip service to the denial of greed and the acquisition of wealth and material possessions, but, all too often, have acquiesced in and even supported this process of exploitation – nowhere has this been clearer than the Catholic Church's identification with the Conquistadors who took control of much of South America, and the Protestant "prosperity theology" so common in the United States. The Jewish tradition saw human beings living in harmony with nature, clearly emphasizing the priority of the second account. Further, as we grow in knowledge we increasingly recognize that the attitude of dominance, mastery and exploitation is in our own worst interests. We end up destroying plants and animals which may be of real help to us in the years ahead, destroying the biosphere, destroying the oceans and even the air we breathe. We have lost any idea of living in harmony with creation and have emphasized exploitation and greed.

The exploitation approach has arisen because human beings have become dissatisfied with having enough and have demanded ever more. Human inventiveness has overcome many problems, not least (at least so far) the problem of very large human populations. However, the move to exploit rather than to conserve, to "conquer" and "master" rather than to "cultivate" and "care for" has been very obvious. It is only in recent years that human beings have realized what they are doing and have begun to take the first very tentative steps to correct the position – or at least to talk about taking such steps. Theologians need to take more seriously the clear facts about the position of human beings within the environment portrayed so clearly by James Lovelock and others and to recognize that their old ways of thinking concentrated on inadequate models.

In the case of animal suffering, the worst excesses have been caused not by animals preying on each other but by human-inflicted suffering. Agreed, one species normally preys on other species and the life of any individual animal is likely to be terminated by the action of some other. The end is, however, relatively quick and up to that point the animal's life would conform to the norm for the animal – a spider would have a spider's natural life, a fox that of a fox, a rabbit that of a rabbit. Only animals kept by humans are

subjected to continuous misery and suffering which goes totally against
the natural order through their whole lives: battery chickens confined
for the whole of their lives to intolerable conditions in which they
can never turn round and never grow feathers; intensively-reared
pigs and veal calves which never see the sky; sheep transported for
hundreds of miles in overcrowded wagons without any water;
Australian cattle wagons which take cattle thousands of miles with
the dead ones being just discarded by the roadside; birds trapped
by their hundreds of thousands in Malta while on migration;
myxomatosis (the white blindness) deliberately introduced into the
rabbit population by men; animals used for cosmetics-testing in
laboratories round the world and so on. Ralph Hodgson put it well
in the following poem:

> T'would ring the bells of heaven
> The wildest peal for years,
> If parson lost his senses
> And people came to theirs
> And he and they together
> Knelt down with angry prayers
> For tame and shabby tigers
> And dancing dogs and bears,
> And wretched blind pit ponies
> And little hunted hares.
>
> (RALPH HODGSON)

Any argument against evolution as a tool for developing the animal
and plant life of the world would need to show what better technique
could be produced to achieve the same ends. It is much easier to
argue against suffering inflicted by human beings on animals and
certainly the second chapter of Genesis has consistently been ignored.
Genesis 2 calls people to "cultivate and care for" animals and plants,
to see themselves as part of the world, and there is little sign that
this is what is done. In all too many cases the only motive is

exploitation with a view to profit. The worst suffering of animals can, therefore, be blamed on the free actions of human beings and we will tackle this issue in the next chapter.

In previous chapters we have seen that God's almighty power is in fact severely limited because of the world he has chosen to create. God has created a world of incredible complexity. It is finely balanced and planned and obeys known physical laws. If human beings are to adapt to their environment, then natural laws must operate regularly and evolutionary forces must be allowed relatively free rein. Human beings must be able to learn, to discover, how the universe works, to adapt to their environment and to adapt the environment to their own needs. The universe is ordered, it is the very opposite of chaos. We have seen that both the two accounts of creation at the beginning of the book of Genesis proclaim God's activity in bringing order out of chaos.

If a true chaotic state of affairs could exist, something that is highly debatable, then matter would behave in a purely random manner. Atoms would group with other atoms at random and would then fall apart, objects would go into and out of existence, there would be no physical laws because they would be changing all the time, there could be no organisms or complex bodies of any sort as, as soon as the component parts came together, they could fly apart again, disintegrate or just go out of existence. True chaos is not just unimaginable, it is impossible. Some physical laws have to operate if there is to be a universe at all. You cannot have gravity working at two different rates at two adjacent places. Light cannot travel at 186,000 miles per second and then suddenly slow to 700 miles per hour. A human being cannot have a body with internal organs surrounded by skin and then suddenly have all the internal organs disintegrate into pink sponge and hang from the flaccid skin! A truly chaotic world is not just a world of nightmares, it is a truly unimaginable world. It is unimaginable because it is not possible.

Even if God did not create from nothing the raw matter from which the universe is formed, this pre-existent raw matter would have to obey certain laws in order to exist at all. Raw matter might, possibly, be held to exist unformed and unmoulded, but if it is raw matter there must be certain basic laws inherent in the matter itself. True, it may be chaotic matter as there may be no design, but there would have to be order in the matter itself. An example might illustrate this. One could imagine stones dumped from a truck in a pile. A sculptor might then take this pile of stone and, by careful fashioning, produce a most beautiful statue from it. One could then say that the sculptor had produced beauty and order out of chaos. However this would not be to say that the stone itself did not obey known natural laws. The stone was made up of certain electrons and neutrons and these behave in an entirely predictable fashion. Because of this the stone remains as stone and can be fashioned by the sculptor. His efforts would not be much use if, halfway through his fashioning, the fundamental composition of the stones altered so that they turned into a liquid!

If there is to be a universe of any sort at all, then this universe must be ordered. Of course, there may be disagreement about the extent of this ordering. Some may hold that the Big Bang was ordered and planned, others that it was the result of chance. No scientist, however, will deny that the Big Bang, from the very instant it occurred, obeyed precise laws which are absolutely regular and which are discoverable by human reason either now or in the future.

The universe is not just ordered in terms of the basic building blocks of matter, it is highly ordered at every stage. The various fundamental forces that hold the universe together remain stable and in balance. Energy can be changed to matter and matter to energy according to precisely calculated formulae. Similarly causes and effects are precisely related. We can say with great precision that, if in a stated set of circumstances under precisely stated conditions, a particular causal sequence is initiated in a predetermined manner, then certain predictable events will result. If I drop a round ball from the top of a very high building then its rate of descent will be precisely calculable; if I send a radio wave to the planet Mars the precise time of its arrival can be calculated; if light from the star Alpha Centauri leaves the star, it will take a precise number of light years to reach the earth; if a billiard ball is hit with a particular force at a certain point and rolls across a surface which has a stated rolling resistance then its movement can be precisely plotted; if two hydrogen atoms are brought together with one oxygen atom water will be produced and so on.

Sometimes, of course, a cause gives rise to unlikely effects, but this is because we are not aware of all the variables operating in the given situation. Science advances in this way, it seeks to isolate the known causes and so to discover the unknown ones.

The process of moulding the world to human needs makes man a little like God. God actually gives man the freedom to make a real difference to earth and even, if we advance so far, to the planets of the solar system and the star systems far distant from us. We have the ability to exercise and to take responsibility but this is entirely dependent on the structure of the universe remaining as it is and being law-abiding.

Generally physical evils are regarded as those evils which adversely affect human beings and which are outside direct human control. These would include the effects of volcanoes, earthquakes, tidal waves, locusts, drought and many illnesses including cancer, smallpox, leprosy and the like. All these produce terrible suffering for human beings as well as for animals.

Physical evils arise because of the natural laws inherent in the structure of the universe. Volcanoes occur because pressure inside the earth's crust becomes so great that it has to be relieved through weak spots. Earthquakes happen because the geological plates on which the earth's crust rests move in relation to each other. If the universe is to be orderly, these results appear inevitable. We have seen that the universe must be orderly if there is to be life as we know it and if human beings are to have the chance to learn. The question that immediately arises is whether the natural laws do, indeed, *have* to be structured like they are. Would it not have been possible to have arranged for different natural laws so that volcanoes do not erupt?

On the face of it, this is highly persuasive. Surely it should be possible for God to have so arranged matters that the inside of the earth was not molten and, therefore, pressure did not arise? Surely it should be possible for God to have so planned the world that the geological plates do not move? If you or I were designing a universe, could we not have made a better job of it so as to avoid these natural disasters?

So far in this book I have tried not to retreat behind mystery or to make any faith claims. Generally theologians retreat behind mystery just at that point when their arguments appear weakest and faith is usually brought in to bolster positions that owe more to dogmatism than careful thought. We are now faced, however, with a clear choice and there is absolutely no way of knowing which choice is correct. We started the second part of this book with a "given", the assumption that there exists a God who created the world and sustains it. This cannot be proved, it rests on a faith claim and is a "given" accepted by Christians, Jews and Muslims. They may, of course, be wrong. Perhaps there is no such God. If believers are philosophic realists (if, in other words, they maintain that the word God refers correctly to the God who created and sustains the universe and who is ontologically independent of it whilst being immanent within it), they must accept the possibility that they could be mistaken in their beliefs. However if we continue with this "given" on which this part of the book rests, then we are faced with the following choice:

Given that a God exists who can correctly be described as personal loving and Almighty, who is three persons in one, and who is conceived as the creator and sustainer of the universe who interacts with his creation and who calls human beings to respond to him in love both for himself and for each other, then either:

1. This universe is the best universe that (a) it is possible to produce given the objectives of God stated above or (b) this is one of a

group of possible universes, any one of which would be one of the best that could be produced.

It is necessary to add the second clause above (i.e. "that this is one of a group of possible universes, any one of which would be one of the best that could be produced") to meet a point made by Richard Swinburne in his book *The Existence of God* (Oxford, 1979). Swinburne denies Leibniz' claim that this is the best of all possible worlds on the basis that a world with one more leaf or some other tiny alteration would be neither better nor worse than this one.

As we have seen, Swinburne sets out four different types of "world groups". Swinburne maintains that this world fits into the fourth of his groups. He considers that death is, in fact, necessary and important and that this is, therefore, exactly the sort of world which God would have reason to create. This does not, however, mean that this is the best of all possible worlds – only that this is one of the best possible worlds.

The necessity for death is due, Swinburne maintains, to the need for human beings to be able to have the possibility of self-sacrifice; to the need for God to trust human beings not to inflict the ultimate degree of harm to each other; to the need for the possibility of the higher virtues (courage, self-sacrifice, bravery, etc.); and to the need for there to be a limit to human life. I find part of Swinburne's argument obscene when he claims that God has set limits to the amount of human suffering because firstly we die after a certain number of years and secondly we pass out when pain passes a certain point. It seems that this is the sort of comment that could only be made by an academic philosopher who has never experienced extreme suffering. However, his basic thesis that this is the type of world that a good God might well have reason to create could be a sound one.

2. God could have produced a better universe if he had set his mind to it or had cared more for human beings and the relief of suffering.

Which of these two alternatives is right cannot be proved. There seems no way of rationally demonstrating that it is necessary to have smallpox, earthquakes, tidal waves, volcanoes and the like in order to have a world in which human freedom and the ability to love are maximized. One could imagine that this may well be necessary, but it may not be. If the universe is, indeed, to be orderly and to obey natural laws, then these natural laws must be allowed to operate. It may well be argued that there is simply no better way of arranging the universe. Any alternative would give rise to other problems which we cannot foresee and which would be worse. However, although this could be maintained, I see no way in which it could be proved. We simply do not have the information to assess all the different ways in which possible universes could be constructed and the different consequences.

Because of this, there seems no alternative but for the believer to rely on a faith decision when it comes to physical evil and to say (bringing together all the statements made so far):

i) I accept the existence of a creator God as previously defined.

ii) I make a supreme value judgement by which I hold that the ultimate purpose and meaning for human existence is to be found only in fellowship with and love of God and living out this love in a life of self-giving love to those around us. For this reason I call God good as God is the ultimate source of everything I value most highly. Evil represents anything that makes it more difficult for individuals to achieve this purpose.

iii) I accept that God is Almighty, but by this I do not mean that God is able to exercise total power over the forces of evil in the world. God's power is shown in weakness. Nothing can separate me from God's love and because of this God can help me to overcome evil even though this may lead to suffering.

iv) I believe that God can act in the world in response to the prayers of believers. God cannot, however, be controlled but he can and even does answer prayers. However, such actions by God are going to be rare and will be sparingly used. We cannot see the possible effects of divine interventions and, in placing our petitions before God, must nevertheless accept that his will should be done as only he can see the implications of any possible action. Prayer therefore involves trust.

v) I am aware of the existence of physical evil and am appalled by the suffering it causes both to humans and animals. Nevertheless, although I cannot prove it, I hold that God could not have created a better universe given his ultimate purposes and that we need to see ourselves as a part of the world with a responsibility for it. I hold this because of the value judgement I make in (ii) above. Because of my belief in and love for this God, I refuse to accept that a world with less suffering due to physical evil could have been created, although I recognize that I am making an assumption here which I cannot justify.

vi) I accept that I could be wrong about all of the above statements but am ready to stake my life on the "if" that I am right. I cannot do more.

We must now turn to consider the problem of moral evil.

THIRTEEN

Moral Evil – Job and Ivan

Happy are those who do not follow the advice of evil men,
    who do not follow the example of sinners . . .
Instead they find joy in obeying the Law of the Lord,
    and they study it day and night . . .
But evil men are not like this at all;
    they are like straw that the wind blows away . . .
    and they are on their way to their doom.

Psalm 1:1, 2, 4, 6

The most extreme sufferings and the worst evil in the world is that which is due to the agency of human beings. Wars throughout the centuries; genocide; abuse and torture of little children; mental cruelty; suffering inflicted on animals and many, many other evils are a central part of the world in which we live. Any human being must feel touched, hurt and outraged by the hardship, suffering and evil around us. It is all too easy for those of us in the West to live closeted lives, well insulated from the extremes of suffering. We even insulate ourselves from death – old and ill people are parcelled out to hospitals, geriatric homes and hospices. We do not talk about death and often try to avoid the real horror of suffering, exercising our choice by switching television channels when pictures come onto our television screens which disturb and upset us.

In the first part of the book, we looked at Ivan Karamazov's charge that the suffering of innocent children is simply not worth any price. If God had to erect the edifice of creation on the tears of one innocent child it is, says Ivan, simply not worth it. The power of Ivan's case comes from the horror and outrage we rightly feel in the face of innocent suffering. We may be able to accept adult suffering, but the extreme suffering of innocent children raises in us such strong feelings of repugnance and outrage that rebellion against the God who would allow this seems the natural course.

Camus, throughout his life, was preoccupied with the question of innocent suffering. Camus believed there was no place for God in a world where suffering and evil were such terrible realities. Camus echoes Ivan's outrage on the lips of one of his characters in a sermon in his novel *The Plague*:

> . . . nothing was ever more important on earth than a child's suffering, the horror it inspires in us, and the reasons we must find to account for it. In other manifestations of life, God made things easy for us and, thus far, our religion has no merit. But in this respect he put us, so to speak, with our backs to the wall. Indeed, we were all up against the wall that plague had built round us, and in its lethal shadow we must work our own salvation.

In the face of extreme evil and suffering our backs are against the wall. We are alone with our fears, with our impotence, with our horror of pain, with our fear of pointlessness and death – we are alone with our anger and our destroyed pride. Humbled, abused, cowed and angry – yet without the resources to be angry.

No one can deny that Christians have taken the existence of evil seriously. Some, of course, have treated evil as something of an academic exercise, but in the present century this option is no longer open to us. With the knowledge of Auschwitz so recent, with the affront to our sensibilities provided by television bringing extreme suffering into our living rooms we have no excuse for ignorance. If we turn our back on suffering it is a voluntary decision on our part, freely entered into. The priest and the Levite turned their backs on the wounded man on the road in Jesus' parable – so, similarly, many of us turn our backs on the sufferings of the world when we fail to engage with their distress, when we fail to feel outrage, when we shut the suffering millions of the world out from our consciousness.

Suffering is taken seriously as a starting point for theology particularly among some of Latin America's liberation theologians. Among many Catholic theologians, the "option for the poor" is no longer a voluntary option, it is a prerequisite for the Christian life. Michael Campbell-Johnson SJ, the Provincial of the British Jesuits who has spent much of his ministry working amongst the poorest of the poor in South America, in an article in the Jesuit journal *The Month* in December 1988 entitled "Can a Conservative be a Christian?" argued that anyone who does not acknowledge the preferential position of the poor cannot rightfully call themselves a Christian.

Liberation theology starts from the undeniable fact of suffering. Possibly the most powerful account of suffering as a starting point for theology comes from Gustavo Gutierrez in his book *On Job* (Orbis Books, 1987). I will draw on Gutierrez in what follows although will modify his conclusion and will use Søren Kierkegaard's approach to Christianity to further illuminate his position.

Gutierrez shows that Job's three friends, his "comforters", work with the model of God's action and justice that was prevailing at the time. God willed things to be as they are and Job's state (having lost all his possessions and family and when he was sitting in ashes plagued by sores all over his body) was due to God's will. According to his comforters, Job must have sinned – otherwise he would not be in his present state. They are clear that God's reward for virtue, honesty and hard work is health, happiness and success while poverty and sickness are the reward for the sinful and lazy.

Job's comforters work with a doctrine of temporal retribution, each individual will get what he or she deserves in this life. This approach is still surprisingly common. Some Evangelical Christians in America proclaim "prosperity theology" and see their wealth as a sure sign of God's love for them for which they give thanks.

Job, although he knows that he is a sinner, maintains that he has done no great crime. He has tried as hard as he can to live an honest and upright life, he has not offended against any of the commandments. He cannot see that his present sufferings can possibly be justified by anything that he has done. He is unambiguous in his view – he does not deserve what he is suffering. Job's cry is echoed by the suffering poor, the innocents around the world.

Job's three friends are competent theologians – they are proclaiming the theological orthodoxy of their time. However, this orthodoxy is mistaken and Job sees their mistake. They are proclaiming an academic and rational approach to suffering and it has nothing to offer to the sufferer. As Gutierrez says:

> In their view, Job's duty is to understand (their) theology and accept it, and apply it to his own situation. Only in this way will he reach interior peace.
>
> (p.27)

His friends want Job to repent, to throw himself on God's mercy. They are convinced that Job's ills must be due to his sin. If he will only acknowledge his sin, God will have mercy on him. Their logic is impeccable. If we accept that God rewards the virtuous and punishes the wicked, then since Job is suffering terrible punishments he must be wicked. He must therefore repent. There is no questioning the rightness of this judgement *if*, and only if, the initial presupposition is accepted. Job, however, will not accept it. He is a righteous man and he will not confess to something he has not done – to do so would be to deny his own integrity. Job rejects his friends' arguments because of his own experience. He acknowledges the rightness of their position when seen from the traditional faith perspective. Thus he says:

> Are you going to keep on talking for ever?
> Do you always have to have the last word?
> If you were in my place and I in yours,
> I could say everything you are saying.

> I could shake my head wisely
>   and drown you with a flood of words.
> I could strengthen you with advice
>   and keep talking comfort to you.
>
> (Job 16:2–5)

The words of his comforters are well and good, but they do not address Job's situation. The same, it may be said, applies to most philosophic talk about the problem of evil. It sets the problem up as an academic problem to be solved by academics. In so doing, it removes the problem from the realm of the existing individual. A perfect example is the approach taken by Aquinas which we looked at in the first part of this book. It is an intellectual's approach and appeals to priests, theologians and academics – it will not help the victim of evil or those who suffer.

Evil must be faced by starting with the position of those who suffer, and that is what Job insists on. He is convinced that he is righteous, or at least as righteous as can reasonably be expected of any human being. He is convinced that his sufferings are not due to God punishing him for his sins. He had a real commitment to the poor and weak, he had never turned away from God and had kept all God's commandments. This conviction should lead to a radical reinterpretation of the way the problem of evil is approached. As Gutierrez says:

> Job's words are a criticism of every theology that lacks human compassion and .contact with reality; the one-directional movement from theological principles to life really goes nowhere . . . His friends try to corner him by claiming that his declaration of innocence amounts to a condemnation of God. Job, put on the defensive, answers that God is not to be justified by condemning the innocent.
>
> (p.30)

Throughout the Old Testament, God demands, through the prophets, justice for the widows, orphans and stranger. He demands that those who follow him care for the poor and the weak. The Old Testament idea of justice went far beyond our use of the word today as fair dealing according to law. It meant caring for the marginalized and defenceless. It was an active and not a passive approach to human existence and it was also radical and very demanding. Jesus affirms and accentuates this tradition. If the poor were being punished by God, this would hardly be the case. Rather, the poor are those who are beloved by God and Jesus separates sheep from goats on the basis of the attitudes of individuals to them.

Towards the end of the book, another friend comes on the scene to talk to Job – this is the young man Elihu. Elihu's approach is different from that of Job's three comforters. He says that Job should not try to understand the reason why God is punishing him – but God clearly does have his reasons. It is wrong to question God. God's reasons may well include bringing troubles to innocent people in order to correct their behaviour and thus bring them closer to him. Thus Elihu says:

> Although God speaks again and again
>> no one pays attention to what he says.
> At night when men are asleep
>> God speaks in dreams and visions.
> He makes them listen to what he says,
>> and they are frightened at his warnings . . .
> God corrects a man by sending sickness
>> and filling his body with pain.
> The sick man loses his appetite,
>> and even the finest food looks revolting.
> His body wastes away to nothing;
>> you can see all his bones.

(Job 33:14–20)

Such explanations for evil are still used by some believers today. Sufferings are sometimes said to be brought by God for the good of human beings. C. S. Lewis took this view. He likened the human being to a statue and pain to the blows the sculptor makes to it to fashion it into perfection. In a similar way pain and suffering are God's blows to us to perfect us and it is through suffering that we are brought closer to him. All these views, however, are based on an approach to God's power that I have argued against in chapter II – that God is in control of all that happens in the world. If this view is rejected, Lewis' analysis of pain and suffering as well as that of Elihu can be rejected as well. Job, of course, does not accept this approach either – it is put forward to be knocked down.

Job wishes to complain against God. Unlike Ivan Karamazov, he does not rebel and reject God. Job continues to believe in and trust God totally although he cannot fathom or understand the situation in which he now finds himself. However, he wants to bring a suit against God, to challenge God. God is his adversary (31:36). He knows God will be the judge of the suit as well as being in the dock, but Job believes that just in bringing the suit he will be justified and will prove to have won his case:

> I would state my case before him,
>   and present all the arguments in my favour.
> I want to know what he would say
>   and how he would answer me.
> Would God use all his strength against me?
>   No, he would listen as I spoke.
> I am honest; I could reason with God;
>   he would declare me innocent once and for all.
>
> (Job 23:4–7)

Ivan Karamazov brings suit against God and himself acts as judge. He condemns God and his only option is suicide. Job wishes to bring suit against God but wants God to be the judge and will continue to trust in God and to live and suffer whatever the outcome may be. The two approaches are similar in their concern for the problem of innocent and undeserved suffering – but radically different in their responses.

Finally God speaks in reply to Job. The fear of God revealing himself is a common feature in the Old Testament. No-one could see God and live and God's holiness was so great that his name could not be uttered. Job is thoroughly nervous at the prospect of confronting God, but his distress and above all his sense of injustice lead him to long for the confrontation more than anything else. His sense of injustice is not just on his own behalf but on behalf of all the weak who suffer. Psalm 73 is a paradigm of the concern for suffering humanity that Job comes to see – that the weak are oppressed and the strong prosper:

> I had nearly lost confidence;
>   my faith was almost gone
> because I was jealous of the proud
>   when I saw that things go well for the wicked.
> They do not suffer pain;
>   they are strong and healthy.
> They do not suffer as other people do;
>   they do not have the troubles that others have.
> And so they wear pride like a necklace
>   and violence like a robe . . .
> They say, "God will not know;
>   the Most High will not find out."
> That is what the wicked are like.
> They have plenty and are always getting more.
> Is it for nothing, then, that I have kept myself pure
>   and have not committed sin?
> O God, you have made me suffer all day long;
>   every morning you have punished me.
>
> (Psalm 73:2–14)

In reply to Job's plea and indictment, God spells out his own greatness in chapters 38 to 40, but as Gutierrez recognizes, he does this in a special way:

> The greatness of God is to be identified less with power than with freedom and gratuitous love – and with tenderness.

(p.68)

The point Gutierrez makes here can be seen as supporting the argument I used in chapter 10 in which I denied God's Almighty power on earth. Gutierrez does not draw this conclusion – he continues to affirm God's power in the world, while I do not, but he emphasizes not this power but rather "fredom and gratuitous love".

God attacks Job's ignorance – who is Job to have any idea of God's purposes and intentions for the world? His human perspective is too impossibly limited:

> Where were you when I made the world?
> if you know so much, tell me about it.
> Who decided how large it would be?
> Who stretched the measuring-line over it?
> Do you know all the answers?

(38:4–5)

> Can you tie the Pleiades together
> or loosen the bonds that hold Orion?
> Can you guide the stars season by season
> and direct the Great and Little Bear?

(38:31–2)

> Who gave the wild donkeys their freedom?
> Who turned them loose and let them roam?
> I gave them the desert to be their home,
> and let them live on the salt plains.

161

The Puzzle of Evil

Will a wild ox work for you?
Is he willing to spend the night in your stable?

(39:5,6,9)

As Gutierrez says when commenting on this passage:

> The speeches say that God indeed has a plan, but it is not one
> that the human mind can grasp so as to make calculations based
> on it and foresee the divine action. God is free; God's love is
> a cause, not an effect that is, as it were, handcuffed.

(p.73)

> God's speeches are a forceful rejection of a purely anthropocentric
> view of creation. Not everything that exists was made to be
> directly useful to human beings, therefore they may not judge
> everything from their point of view.

(p.74)

Human beings are as nothing before God. Human rationality cannot
judge God, it can only accept obedience to God's will. Job recognizes
this and falls silent. God has not actually answered Job's challenge
– rather he has shown Job that though his questions may be valid
he is not in a position to question God. So Job falls silent:

> I feel my littleness: what reply shall I give?
>   I had better lay my hand over my mouth,
> I have spoken once, I shall not speak again;
>   I have spoken twice, I have nothing more to say.

(40:4–5)

Job's last resort is to surrender to the divine love which he has always
been aware of. However, this is a surrender that, as Kierkegaard puts
it, sets reason aside in the interest of faith. It accepts in love, without
questioning why and without trying to make sense or to understand.

Throughout the book of Job, his comforters and Job himself are trying to use reason to understand the ways of God and the reason for Job's evil state.

Kierkegaard would have explained what is happening in terms of paradox, the paradox of the goodness of Job combined with his extreme suffering. When reason meets with paradox there are, Kierkegaard says, two alternatives – either for reason to assert itself and in this case reason will find offence in the paradox and reject it, or for reason to set itself aside and for the individual to accept the paradox in faith. This was how Kierkegaard, in his book *Philosophic Fragments*, contrasted the two possible approaches to the claim that Jesus was both God and man. There are two responses, faith and offence. The latter sees reason as reigning supreme, and reason cannot comprehend the paradox. The former accepts the limits of reason.

The same, I maintain, applies in the case of Job. The whole book is the story of Job's attempt to understand his fate with the aid of reason and he fails. It is only when he is confronted with the presence of God (not, it must be emphasized, with any intellectual answers), when he recognizes the presence of absolute Love, that he sets reason aside and embraces God without question and without condition.

A similar point can be seen as being made by the writer of Psalm 73:

> Is it for nothing, then, that I have kept myself pure
>   and have not committed sin?
> O God you have made me suffer all day long;
>   every morning you have punished me . . .
> I tried to think this problem through,
>   but it was too difficult for me . . .
> When my thoughts were bitter
>   and my feelings were hurt,
> I was as stupid as an animal;
>   I did not understand you.
> Yet I always stay close to you,
>   and you hold me by the hand . . .

The Puzzle of Evil

What else have I in heaven but you?
   Since I have you, what else could I want on earth?
My mind and my body may grow weak,
   But God is my strength; he is all I need.

(Psalm 73:13–26)

"I tried to think this problem through, but it was too difficult for me" expresses precisely the inability of reason to comprehend the paradox, whether this be the paradox of the incarnation or the paradox of a loving God who allows innocent suffering. Finally the Psalmist sets reason aside: "I was as stupid as an animal; I did not understand you" and rests entirely in trust in God: "Yet I always stay close to you, and you hold me by the hand."

This point is fundamental. Today most philosophy operates in a Kantian framework which makes reason supreme. It was not for nothing that Kant's most important book dealing with religion was entitled *Religion within the limits of reason alone*. For most philosophers in the British and American analytic tradition reason reigns supreme. Since rationally it no longers makes sense to believe in the God of traditional Christianity, revisionary accounts are put forward which reinterpret Christian faith within a framework that reason can comprehend.

At the very heart of Christianity, however, is the Absolute Paradox of Jesus who is both fully God and fully man. This is something that reason cannot grasp and yet Christianity proclaims it as ultimate truth. As we saw in a previous chapter, Pilate asked Jesus, "What is truth?" and the demand was for truth that could be proved, that could be demonstrated. The absurdity of the question was that it was addressed to Jesus – who himself was the Truth. If Pilate could not recognize the Truth when confronted by it, there is nothing more to be said. The same applies to the individual being confronted with the claim that Christ was the God-Man. The choice is then either offence – or faith.

Job faced the same choice. Only when reason came to an end,

when he was confronted by the paradox, when his reasoning abilities failed him and when, in their absence, he came into the presence of God, could he make the decision: offence – or faith. Ivan Karamazov chose offence, Job chose faith.

We are then faced with a choice when it comes to the problem of human suffering. We can certainly blame such suffering on human free actions – we can, in other words, make use of the Free Will Defence which we looked at in chapter 3. We cannot, however, rationally decide whether to side with Ivan Karamazov or not. Is the suffering of the weak, the suffering of the innocent and the cries of the afflicted worth whatever God intends for creation? Is the Christian claim that individuals are free to enter into a love relationship with God which will continue after death worth the tears of the children in Auschwitz? There are two approaches:

1. That of Ivan which says, "No, it is not worth it." This approach leads, ultimately, to despair. Ivan rebels and has no hope for the future – suicide is the only way forward. As Camus recognized, with the death of God everything becomes permissible and Ivan's approach led eventually to Stalin and Hitler's death camps. Human beings became the only yardstick for right and wrong, they end in believing in nothing, and the consequences of this have been all too clear.

2. That of Job, which says, "I cannot see how it is worth it and I am horrified and appalled by the suffering of the innocents and will set out to combat it as God has told me to do. I cannot understand how God could allow such suffering but in the end I rest on trust in God – a trust that cannot understand."

A choice has to be made between these two positions. If anything, Ivan's position is more rational. As we saw in the first part of this book, there is no rational way of answering him, just as Job could find no rational answer to his own innocent suffering and the suffering of the poor, the weak and the marginalized. Faith and trust in the power of Love goes beyond reason. It will rest on a fundamental value judgement which cannot be rationally justified.

Added to this, we must also recognize the limitation of God's power in the world which was argued for in chapter 10. Gutierrez and the Book of Job both maintain that God could have altered Job's position if he had wished to do so. Job's problem was that he did not do so. If, however, the world is at least partly outside God's control and if God's powers are strictly limited, then God's ability to intervene is also limited. The real paradox is, then, that God should have allowed Satan to do what he did to Job. It is vital to recognize that all Job's injuries were inflicted by Satan, who acted with God's permission because God was convinced of Job's righteousness and ability to withstand the tests Satan would impose. The real problem is why God should have allowed Satan to act in this way. If God is really wholly good, how could he allow his follower to be so ill-used? The same cry goes up from suffering humanity today and the alternatives are to choose between Ivan's response and the trust of Job himself.

Still, however, the question "why" should rightly plague us. Still we feel pressed to enquire further into the nature of these dark forces that are seemingly able to thwart God's will. Still we feel the need to probe what it means to talk of the Devil. It is to this issue that we turn in the next chapter.

Before this, however, we can add one further statement to those to which the believer has to be committed:

The suffering of innocents, the evils inflicted by the strong on the weak, the cries of the marginalized and outcasts appal me. I know I can either follow Ivan Karamazov and reject God or follow Job and hold fast to him even though I cannot understand how any eventual purpose for human beings or creation as a whole can be worth the suffering that innocents have to undergo. Because of the central value judgement that I have made, I will continue to trust in God and in the meanwhile will fight to do as God intended, namely to overcome injustice and to identify with the poor and the weak who are most beloved of God.

Two problems remain. The first is what it means to talk of the Devil and the second what consequences this understanding of the problem of evil has for the Christian. We must now turn to these in order.

FOURTEEN

The Devil and All His Works

> Why do you boast, great man, of your evil? . . .
> You make plans to ruin others;
>   your tongue is like a sharp razor.
>   You are always investing lies.
> You love evil more than good,
>   and falsehood more than truth.
> You love to hurt people with your words, you liar!
>
> Psalm 52:1, 2–4

In *God, Jesus and Belief* (Blackwell, 1984), Stewart Sutherland draws a comparison between the temptation of Jesus in the wilderness and his prayer in the garden of Gethsemene. He rightly points out that most modern theologians can make sense of the temptation stories without bringing in the idea of a personal Devil who tempted Jesus. Jesus in the desert is depicted as wrestling with real possibilities about how his life was to be lived and his temptation does not require the presence of "The Devil". Although many believers would accept this, Sutherland points out that when they move to consideration of Jesus' prayer in the garden of Gethsemene, they still want to retain belief in a personal God and Sutherland, very reasonably, makes the point that if the temptations can be explained without the Devil, so Jesus' prayer in Gethsemene can be explained without resorting to talk of a personal God. In Gethsemene, Jesus was wrestling with real possibilities, with decisions he had to make about whether to give up his teaching, whether to run away or whether to face the consequences of his ministry. He could have escaped, he could have compromised but instead, after prayer, he decided to be true to his vision and to refuse to allow the fear of death to trivialize the life he had lived.

Sutherland is right to recognize that, today, talk of the Devil has almost been abandoned. A central problem with such language is the caricature picture with which medieval paintings have provided us. Talk of the Devil readily conjures up pictures of horns and a tail surrounded by malevolent imps and fiery furnaces. It is not surprising that in the modern age people dismiss belief in such a myth. This picture is only a caricature, however, and dismissal of the caricature need not entail dismissal of the reality of evil.

God, in many medieval paintings, was depicted as an old man with a white beard. Blake's portrait or Michaelangelo's painting on the ceiling of the Sistine Chapel are good examples. No serious theologian or philosopher, however, regards God in such a light. Muslims do not allow pictures of Allah and the Jews scarcely even mention Yahweh's name. God is far beyond human comprehension. Central, indeed, to the theology of St Thomas Aquinas is the idea of God as beyond understanding. Language about God may be correctly and truthfully used but this does not mean that we know what it is for this language to be true when applied to God. God, for Aquinas, does not have a body and is outside space and time. Pictures of God do not, therefore, even begin to capture his reality. The same, although to a lesser degree, may apply to the force of evil.

In the discussion which follows I will not use the term "Devil" because of its connotations and will instead use "the forces of evil". The central question is whether there are such forces and, if so, whether they are entirely locatable within the human psyche.

According to Nietzsche, when a bad person does something wrong, he thinks it is grounded in the power of Satan or evil forces – those forces greater than human beings who seek our spiritual destruction. By contrast, when a good person does something wrong, he thinks of it as an action which is not living up to his true character and potential. So to be bad is not to be living to one's full potential (the Thomist influence here is clear). If, therefore, the good person commits bad acts, he rejects the acts and resolves to do better, to be stronger in the future. The evil person, however, cowers beneath the power of dark forces who have mastered him and which he cannot overthrow. The good person sees a distinction between bad things which good people should not do and good which they should do. The bad person, by contrast sees the good as the weaker of two opposing forces – the more powerful of which, Satan, can rule him. The latter position, of course, denies human responsibility and an individual who accepts this view sees himself as under the control of forces greater than himself.

Nietzsche considered that "evil" must stand for a source of power independent of the human. Many people do indeed believe in such a power. Stories of demons, witches, devils, vampires, ghosts, goblins and wicked spirits are common all over the world. Many, many horror films today depend on belief in the existence of such creatures and depict evil as having a supernatural source. If you go into any video store you will see shelves of horror movies, all of which depict the power of evil as being very real and as something that can be tapped. Cases of ritual Satanic abuse of children have recently had headline treatment in America and Europe. Many social workers consider such rituals to be a cloak for sexual deviancy, yet the idea that other forces may be at work needs theological examination. There is something deep in the human psyche which accepts the reality of these forces.

In Michael Gelven's book *Spirit and Existence – A philosophical enquiry into the meaning of spiritual existence* (HarperCollins, 1990), he considers Nietzsche's approach. However he denies that there is any external power source representing a force of evil. Thus he says:

> Nietzsche is correct that evil is thought of as a power and indeed an alien power. But it is not an external power. It is rather the power which we ourselves may become and which permanently alters us.

Anyone who has been through psychotherapy or psychoanalysis will know that the human psyche is deep indeed and in its depths often lurk dark realities – sometimes garnered in during childhood days and working their destructive effect on the individual unseen and unknown. These dark realities are real and have great power. They are primeval and awesome forces which can easily seem to shape and control our lives. It is plausible to think of the power of evil in terms of these forces. On this view, Christianity seeks to free us from the power of these primeval forces and to restore us to human wholeness, a wholeness unmarred by the psychological scars that all human beings bear.

The days are long gone when a power of evil was seen to lurk along the Christian's way, ready to seduce him or her from the paths of righteousness. Most believers have moved on beyond these supposed primitive ideas, and belief in the forces of darkness has generally been consigned to the dustbin of history. The dismissal of the power of evil or its reduction to forces operating within the human psyche is often mirrored by a dismissal of God, as we have seen in the case of Stewart Sutherland. Once again, many modern theologians take this approach. They consider the idea of a creator God who interacts with and sustains the world too problematic and, therefore, they seek to give talk about God a different reality – found, possibly, within the believing community. Talk about God can be held to point us towards a better way of living life and we can be encouraged to find an ethical transcendence of self. Apart from Sutherland himself, Don Cupitt, Dewi Phillips and many others take this approach. I have already said that I do not. I started the second half of this book with a faith claim which could not be proved to be true, a faith claim in the traditional Christian idea of God who exists independently of the universe, who can rightly be described as personal and loving, who interacts with the world and into whose presence I will go when I die. I am sailing under Augustine's banner – "I believe in order that I may understand". I fully accept that this premise may be rejected as it is based on no rational grounds but my purpose in the second half of this book is to try to set out what can be said in the light of the existence of extreme evil and suffering, given that God exists.

If, therefore, one starts from the assumption that God exists, then it is also possible to accept that a force of evil is not an *a priori* impossibility. Indeed, I want to argue not just that the existence of such a force of evil cannot be ruled out, but that it may well be necessary. The power of the forces of evil has, until very recently, always been realized. The Gospels are clear in their affirmation of the forces of darkness. In spite of this, however, many Christians today are highly selective in their beliefs.

Most Christians still believe in God (I say "most" because an increasing minority of priests and theologians find nothing but difficulty with the traditional view of a loving God who really does care for each individual). However, there are two crucial features of traditional Christian teaching which many of those who affirm that God exists still reject: the first is belief in the existence of a force of evil independent of the human psyche and the second is belief in judgement after death.

Belief in any sort of judgement after death is played down for sound and compassionate reasons. Few people like to take this idea seriously. After all, we as individuals may feel that we may not fare favourably if we are judged by God against his standards. Also, there has been so much emphasis on the idea that God is a God of love that many have felt that this rules out the possibility of judgement. How, it may be asked, could a loving God possibly judge us? How, if God really loves us, could he possibly consign us to a place which is permanently excluded from his presence? These are reasonable questions – the only problem is that both the Gospels and the traditional teaching of all the mainstream Churches is that this is exactly what God *does* do!

Christians are, then, faced with an alternative. They can either abandon those beliefs that do not seem fair and reasonable or which do not suit their present tastes, or they can hold to traditional belief.

This is a stark choice. The arguments of Don Cupitt, Gareth Moore, Grace Jantzen, David Jenkins, Nicholas Lash, Dewi Phillips, Maurice Wiles and others appear to be persuasive. They may be right (well, some of them. They cannot all be right as they all seem to be more or less different). Reasonability seems on their side. The trouble is that Christianity has never claimed to be reasonable. As St Paul says, it is "Foolishness to the Greeks". The Greeks, of course, were the philosophers of their day and Tertullian asked what Athens had to do with Jerusalem. The resurrection appeared to be folly to many who heard about it and throughout the centuries most people have paid lip service to the whole message of Christianity but few have ever really been willing to take it on board.

If God exists as traditionally defined, then the idea of a judgement after death may not be pleasant but it is entirely plausible. *If* there is such a God and *if* God created the world in order that human beings should be free to enter into a relationship with him, or not as they choose, then a judgement after death is essential. To be sure, this judgement need not be portrayed in crude terms. The judgement may well depend on the sort of people into which we have made ourselves. We can either choose, by our thoughts and actions, to make ourselves into people who can love and care for each other and for God and who put self-interest into second place, or else we can become preoccupied with self, give in to evil and thereby turn our backs on love. It is always easy, more comfortable and above all safer not to love.

God may love every individual, always. However, in this life people have choices to make and by these choices determine the sort of people they are to become. When human beings die, their characters are fixed – they have made themselves who they are and, sadly, many of them will have made themselves into people who are incapable of love, who are incapable of caring for others or relating to God. We will have judged ourselves and the last place we may want to be is in the presence of God. In her book *The Prince of Darkness*, Joan O'Grady makes this point clearly:

John Scotus Eurigena, in the ninth century, said that hell was a metaphor, not a locality. Hell was the permanent understanding, after death (and it was the permanence that was important) that you have got what you want; that is you have achieved alienation from God in the fulfilment of your own desires, instead of what God wants for you, which is your union with him.

This idea of hell does not envisage a Devil imposing punishments and torment, yet it could well include the idea of a malignant spirit, opposed to the good of mankind, enticing human beings by false suggestion and creating influences that would prevent them finding their real good. So disbelief in the Hell of physical punishment, portrayed by medieval preachers and those of later periods, does not necessarily mean disbelief in the presence of a malevolent and hostile intelligence. It has clearly never been necessary to believe in the existence of a goat-like, cloven-hoofed creature in order to acknowledge the possible existence of an enemy of God and man.

(pp.48–9)

It is important to remember that in the traditional story of the Fall of mankind, Satan brought to the world not only sin but also death. It could, therefore, be that any evil force might not so much want to drag human souls down to some fiery torment but rather to ensure that they do not survive death at all. As Joan O'Grady says: "It would seem to follow that true immortality has to be earned. St Augustine said that this world was a world of soul making" (p.50). Perhaps, on this basis, human immortality is not automatic but something that has to be worked for.

The idea of judgement after death or at least the decisive effect of the kind of life individuals live in this world on what happens in the next, is not an optional extra in Christianity which can be discarded because it gives rise to unpleasant thoughts. It is, rather, a central part of traditional Christian belief and of God's purposes. Without any idea of judgement, the idea of God creating human beings and giving them freedom becomes pointless. If a creator God is posited and if human freedom is accepted, then the way this freedom is used must have consequences. At the end of an individual's life the fact of judgement and of the decisive character of the way we live our lives means that human beings *matter* as individuals. A denial of a final judgement is a denial of our worth, a denial of our importance and our irreduceable value.

Once a life after death and the idea of judgement is accepted then the possibility of a heavenly realm is opened. If people survive death as individuals, as Christianity has always proclaimed, then it follows that those who have died are now alive. They exist as individuals in the presence of God. This is what talk about heaven means and has always meant. It means that this world is not all there is – there is a transcendent order, a transcendent realm. Such talk is not popular and is readily dismissed but unpopularity does not falsify the claim.

If there is a life after death, then not only does talk of heaven become a possibility once more but, more important for our present purposes, there can be talk of hell or at least of permanent alienation from God. Similarly if God exists as traditionally defined, then the possibility of a force of evil similarly existing is also opened up. Traditionally, the idea of the Fall of angels from heaven has been used to make sense of hell and talk of the Devil. However such a Fall is not really a scriptural idea. It did not enter into Old Testament thinking in any major way and it was only from the fifth century B.C. onwards that the idea of Satan as an evil power began to be taken seriously. What the Fall does express, however, is the conviction that God created only good and this good then fell from its perfect state in rebellion against God. Indeed later writers (starting with Origen and later Aquinas) were to see the chief feature of Satan and the Devils as being pride. They refused to submit to God, they wished to be autonomous and to make their own way without acknowledging their dependence on God. To know and follow God requires humility, it requires a recognition of our weakness – pride prevents these steps being taken which is why it has always been held to be the most serious sin.

The New Testament has many references to the power of evil and of the Devil. These include:

He was a murderer from the beginning and abode not in the truth, because there is no truth in him. When he speaketh a lie, he speaketh of his own; for he is a liar and the father of it.

(John 8:44)

The Devil is meant to have entered into Judas (John 13:2 and 27) and Jesus says that Peter was in danger of falling into Satan's hands (Luke 22:31). John's Gospel describes Satan as "the prince of this world" (12:31 and 14:30).

Christ came to destroy the power of the devil.

(Hebrews 2:14ff)

Be sober, be diligent; because your adversary, the Devil, as a roaring lion, walketh about, seeing whom he may devour.

(1 Peter 5:8)

Put on the whole armour of God, that ye may be able to stand against the wiles of the Devil. For we wrestle not against flesh and blood, but against principalities, against powers, against the rulers of the darkness of this world, against spiritual wickedness in high places.

(Ephesians 6:11–12)

And the great dragon was cast out, that old serpent, called the Devil and Satan, which deceiveth the whole world; he was cast out into the earth and his angels were cast out with him.

(Revelation 12:9)

Subsequent Christian writers stressed the malevolent power of the Devil and they wrestled with how to affirm this without limiting God. It is only very recently that the idea of a real and positive force of evil existing independently of the human psyche has been questioned.

Some Christians believed that Satan had created matter and that, therefore, the whole of the physical world was evil. There was an important Christian heresy that affirmed this – Manicheanism (already referred to in chapter 2). The Council of Braga was called in A.D. 563 specifically to deny this doctrine and it laid down that Satan was created by God and fell through the exercise of the free will that had been given to him. Pope Gregory said that Satan was lord of this world (a similar point to the one I made above in relation to Jesus' temptation in the wilderness) – however this was because Satan was held to be the lord of sinful humanity.

Whether or not there exists a force of evil independent of the human psyche cannot be proved. There is no doubt at all of the power within the human psyche of such a force. It is a force that seeks to draw us down, to draw individuals away from that of which they are capable and thus to draw them away from God. It can be argued that whether the force exists independently of the human psyche does not matter. Joan O'Grady concludes her book as follows:

> All that is certain is that lies and false suggestion have the power to destroy us, if we let them, and so it is they, from wherever they come, that constitute the dark enemy of our world – the enemy who, from time immemorial, has been called the Prince of Darkness.
>
> (p.151)

On this basis, the existence or otherwise of a force of evil is not important. Excellent though Joan O'Grady's analysis of the history of the idea of Satan is, I do not agree with her conclusion. It is important whether such a force exists.

The traditional Christian position is straightforward and persuasive. It holds that there are two realms, the earthly and the heavenly. If there is, indeed, a heavenly realm then there is no reason at all why free will should not exist in this realm as well as on earth. Agreed, there is an assumption here, but it is not a ridiculous assumption *if* human beings do indeed rise from the dead. If there is to be a life after death, then this life is not on earth and must be somewhere else. A heavenly realm is, then, not just a possibility but a necessity as well. If there is such a realm with free will, then the existence of a force of evil, representing those heavenly forces that have turned away from God, follows logically from the initial assumptions.

As we saw in chapter 2, St Augustine and St Thomas Aquinas maintained that the devils were good at least to the extent that they existed and their existence depended on God. However they were evil in that they had turned away from God and therefore fell far short of what God intended for them. They were fallen angels and their fallen state was not just the fall from heaven to hell but the fall from their original angelic perfection into a lesser state which still included existence but which denied all the higher attributes and aims that God had intended for them. Their chief feature was pride, the wish to attain the highest purposes by their own endeavour without submission to God.

The position that traditional Christianity has always maintained is that the world is not wholly in God's control because it is in the grip of transcendent forces that are dependent on God for their existence but have used their God-given freedom to rebel against God. In chapter 10, I argued for this position and that the New Testament portrays the forces of evil as having considerable power. This does not mean, however, that these forces can manipulate or exercise any control without the free assent and connivance of human beings. Any evil forces can persuade and cajole, but they cannot determine how human beings act, at least until such point as individuals give up their free will to these forces, as depicted in Goethe's *Faust*. Even in such cases, the possibility of redemption, of forgiveness and starting afresh, is always open, although this can become progressively more difficult as individuals become set in their ways, accustomed to giving in to pride, malice, envy, jealousy, lies and selfishness and thus less inclined to turn themselves round. The power individuals who have chosen to follow God have in response is – drawing on the strength provided by their relationship with God – to "shine as lights in the world", to act as leaven in the lump, to try to stand out against the powers of darkness and to let their individual example as well as their love and commitment to others serve as an inspiration to those around them. This is a radical view but it is one that is faithful both to the New Testament and also to the mainstream Christian tradition.

To the extent that human beings turn away from God, they may open themselves to transcendent forces that can increase their control over them. These forces have no power over any individual if he or she commits the whole of his or her life to God, but few are willing to do this. For the vast majority of people, these forces will never make themselves felt. Most people are so preoccupied with their own lives and their own interests and effectively ignore God so completely that the actions of evil forces are not relevant. Those who *may* be aware of them are those who are closest to God. People who are so preoccupied with their own concerns that spiritual struggle is wholly alien to them will have made their own gods (of money, power, reputation, self-interest, pleasure, etc.) and the spiritual realm is simply disregarded. If there are evil forces, such people are of little concern.

Christianity calls individuals to freedom, to a freedom that they may not be aware that they have. Although it is unfashionable today, Christianity has always talked of human beings as being in bondage to the powers of darkness and of sin. Christ came to save people from their sins and the cumulative effects they have had on them and this means freeing them from the bondage of the past so that they can start again.

The existence of a force of evil independent of the human psyche will have profound consequences for any understanding of God's power in the world and its limitations. David Hume (*Dialogues concerning Natural Religion*, chapters 10, 11) and John Mill (*Three Essays on Religion*) convincingly argued that one could not arrive at a wholly good and all-powerful God from the facts in the world. If God's power in the world is limited, to what is its limitation due? In chapter 10 I argued against cosmic dualism or the idea that matter was not created by God. Instead I maintained that God's power was necessarily limited by various factors including the finely balanced forces that make up the physical universe. In addition, it seems prefectly reasonable for the Christian to maintain that the free will of heavenly beings also limits God's power. In other words, the existence of a force of evil active in the world imposes limits on God's ability to bring his purposes about.

Christians are, therefore, engaged in a real struggle on the side of God and the good against the forces of evil. The only assurance is that each individual who wholly turns to God cannot, in this life or after death, be separated from him, but there is no assurance at all about the great mass of mankind. Christianity has always maintained that the struggle against evil *matters*, that each individual will survive death and what happens to him or her after death will depend on how life is lived. The idea of salvation encapsulates this insight and holds that the kingdom of heaven, the heavenly kingdom, is available to and open to all mankind but that the way into it is hard and stony. It is not an easy or comfortable option.

To understand the limitations that the forces of evil impose on God's ability to act in the world, theologians have developed the idea of original sin. We are clear today that the sins of the fathers are indeed visited on subsequent offspring. Children who are beaten or sexually abused or who come from broken homes are almost certain to suffer severe psychological damage and this damage will affect their treatment of their own children and so the original disorder is often passed down through the generations. On a smaller scale, parental disinterest or scorn will affect the grown adult throughout his or her life. Evil and the powers of darkness have become deeply embedded in the human psyche and Christians need to take a stand against these forces and to bring light to a world where darkness reigns.

People are called to absorb evil, not to retaliate. To turn the other cheek, to walk the extra mile, to forgive not seven times but seventy times seven, not to harbour resentment, to look always for the beam in their own eyes, not to judge others and to love everyone. This is a call to absorb the world's evil. It is a radical departure from the Old Testament idea of revenge. "An eye for an eye and a tooth for a tooth" is a recipe for perpetuating evil. The Christian, by contrast, absorbs, or should absorb, evil into him or herself by not letting it determine his or her reactions. The power of love is the power to stop evil in its tracks. This is, of course, incredibly demanding. Our natural human reaction is to "get even", to seek revenge. A rejection of this path is not easy, but it is the only way of overcoming the cycle of past pride, selfishness, arrogance and jealousy.

A picture thus emerges which is faithful to the New Testament insight – a world in which the forces of self-concern largely dominate, in which God's ability to act is severely constrained, in which there is the possibility of forces of evil independent of the human psyche occasionally being at work. This in turn leads to a challenging vision, to the need for spiritual warfare, to the need for the individual to fight against those forces which are at work within his or her own psyche, within the community and in the transcendent realm.

We need to recognize that loving another person can liberate them. If we loved and cared for one another properly then many of the scars that affect our personalities would not exist. Unfortunately the word love is overused. It is often employed to describe a transitory, erotic feeling. Even the love that leads to marriage rarely survives and even parental love often turns into disapproval. For people to really love others, to commit themselves to others and to give them their time and their energy even if they may not like them is incredibly demanding and draining. Few people are aware of being really loved and cared for and it is probably the realization that God loves the individual that is the single most startling and significant factor in the individual's turn round from the dark to the light. It is, however, only once we have experienced being loved unconditionally that we can take this love out to others, it is only when we realize what it means to be forgiven that we can really forgive others. The love from God and the relationship this brings is the starting point in the fight back against the forces of evil because when we live in the presence of God we are bound to love and not to be critical. This is put well by Evelyn Underhill:

> . . . Christ never criticized any but the respectable and pious, with everyone else his thought went like a shaft of delight straight to something he could admire – the love of the prostitute, the meekness of the publican, the faith of the centurion, the confidence of the penitent thief – all things which irradiate and save humanity. Love looks for these first and one reason why Christ gives us rest, is that in his presence we are bound to love – not to criticize.
>
> (quoted in *The Bridge is Love*, Ed. Elizabeth Bassett, p.50)

The power of evil, then, is real and it cannot be overturned by force. There is really only one remedy against it and that is love, just as there is only one source for the strength to put this remedy into effect in our day-to-day lives.

Summary

It does not seem to be necessary for a Christian to affirm the existence of a force of evil ontologically distinct from the human psyche, but it does seem likely that such a force may exist. If this existence is a reality, then the first move of any such force would logically be to convince everyone of its non-existence. Whether or not there is such a force, the power of evil remains a great and terrifying reality – to be found at the very least within our own psyche, and maybe beyond it as well. The fight against this reality, the struggle to master and overcome it, is one that should last any individual his or her whole lifetime and one which may never be finally overcome this side of the grave. The worst temptation of all is to believe that no struggle is necessary and that the fight against evil, whatever its form, is a thing of the past. Once this view is taken, evil has triumphed.

FIFTEEN

The Challenge of Freedom

I have chosen to be obedient;
    I have paid attention to your judgements . . .
I want to obey your commands;
    Give me new life, for you are righteous . . .
The heart of your law is truth,
    and all your righteous judgements are eternal.

Psalm 119:30, 40, 160

In the previous chapters I have argued for various positions which are part of the mainstream Christian heritage and yet which today are not widely accepted. One central question remains to be tackled and that is the issue of human freedom. Such freedom is generally assumed but its consequences are rarely explored and yet Christianity depends on human beings having genuine freedom, with the ability to make choices that are not wholly determined by their nature, education or background.

It is highly debatable whether human beings are as free as they like to suppose. We have already seen (chapter 5) that Ivan Karamazov, in Dostoyevsky's book *The Brothers Karamazov*, maintained that human freedom was simply not worth the price of innocent suffering. His horrific examples of the suffering of children appal most readers and our newspapers and television provide ample evidence of similar cases today. We have already seen that there are no simple answers to Ivan's challenge and that Job's response may be the only way forward for a believer. However Ivan's challenge does not stop there, it is extended and developed in the story he tells his brother Alyosha, the story of the Grand Inquisitor (pp. 294–305 Penguin ed.).

The Challenge of Freedom

The scene is Seville in Spain at the height of the Inquisition. Jesus returns a second time into the hot streets and lanes of the southern city just at that moment when, a day before, nearly a hundred heretics had been burnt by the Inquisition in the presence of the Cardinal, the King and the entire Court. The huge crowd recognizes Jesus and press round him shouting "Hosanna". He walks among them exuding love with a gentle smile of compassion on his face. He cures some and raises a woman from the dead. The Grand Inquisitor, the aged and venerable Cardinal himself, comes out and sees the scene. The Inquisitor, above all others, represents the Church triumphant, the worldwide Church which proclaims its knowledge of the truth and is determined to stamp out error – at whatever cost. He recognizes what is happening and sends his guards to arrest Jesus. The crowd makes way for them and Jesus is brought before him. The Inquisitor speaks to Jesus and his speech represents a devastating attack on Christianity – an attack which has, however, largely been ignored by theologians and philosophers.

The Inquisitor holds that Jesus' demands were unrealistic and his supposed gift of freedom amounted to an intolerable burden with which people could not cope. Jesus did not really love people – if he had, he would have given them the three things offered "by the great and wise spirit" in the desert: *Bread* representing their material needs, *Political authority* that would have taught them how to live and the *miracles* that would have ensured their obedience:

"Do you know that ages will pass and mankind will proclaim in its wisdom and science that there is no crime and, therefore, no sin, but that there are only hungry people. 'Feed them first and then demand virtue of them!' – that is what they will inscribe on their banner which they will raise against you and which will destroy your temple . . . No science will give them bread as long as they remain free. But in the end they will lay their freedom at our feet and say to us, 'We don't mind being your slaves so long as you feed us!' They will, at last, realize themselves that there cannot be enough freedom and bread for everyone, for they will never, never be able to let everyone have his fair share . . . You promised them bread from heaven, but can it compare with earthly bread in the eyes of the weak, always ignoble and vicious race of man? And if for the sake of the bread from heaven, thousands and tens of thousands will follow you, what is to become of the millions and scores of millions of creatures who will not have the strength to give up the earthly bread for the sake of heavenly? Or are only the thousands of the great and strong dear to you . . . No, to us the weak, too, are dear. They are vicious and rebellious, but in the end they will become obedient too . . . we shall tell them that we do your bidding and rule in your name."

Jesus offered only that which was enigmatic and vague. He offered a call to follow God which was incredibly demanding and with which none but a tiny few could possibly cope. The Inquisitor continues:

"You hungered for freely given love and not for the servile raptures of the slave before the might that has terrified him once and for all . . . Had you respected him less, you would have asked less of him, and that would have been more like love, for his burden would have been lighter."

The Church, or at least Church leaders, recognized this and, loving people more than Jesus ever did, gave people what they really wanted in return for their obedience. In so doing, the Church served Satan rather than God, it deceived people but it did this out of love because it reduced Jesus' demand to a manageable level. It gave them what they wanted – magic, mystery and authority and looked forward to a world of peace and security where freedom has been relinquished and where people were obedient.

The Jesus figure in Ivan Karamazov's story does not reply to the

Inquisitor, indeed he does not say a word throughout the story Dostoyevsky's Ivan finishes his story in this way:

> ... when the Inquisitor finished speaking he waited some time for the prisoner's reply. His silence distressed him ... The old man would have liked him to say something, however bitter and terrible. But he suddenly approached the old man and kissed him gently on his bloodless, aged lips. That was all his answer. The old man gave a start. There was an imperceptible movement at the corners of his mouth; he went to the door, opened it and said to him: "Go, and come no more – don't come at all – never, never!" And he let him out into the dark streets and lanes of the city. The prisoner went away.
>
> (p.308)

Finally Ivan says of the Inquisitor that: "The kiss glowed in his heart, but the old man sticks to his idea."

This story has profound insights into what is wrong with the way the Christian message is sometimes presented today and with the understanding of what Christianity is about. I have argued that God is not in control in the world, that individual human beings are called to stand out against generally accepted values in the world in spite of opposition, rejection, scorn, misunderstanding and suffering. The Inquisitor paints the message that Jesus came to bring as centrally requiring a free response from individuals and claims that this is challenging and difficult.

The Inquisitor is right to say that if Jesus had accepted any of the three temptations, which are remarkable in the manner in which they encapsulate human desires, by catering to people's material needs; by performing miracles or by taking political authority, a kingdom of peace could have been quickly established and massive suffering avoided. Anyone wishing to defend Jesus' action needs to accept this challenge.

Judaism at the time of Jesus had institutionalized religion. The

Law was no longer regarded as a means to bring people closer to God but as an end in its own right. Jewish rabbis had worked hard over many generations to perfect and codify a set of rules for the life of the people of Israel. This is one reason why Jesus scandalized the Pharisees when he broke the rules, for instance by plucking corn on the Sabbath, by not washing before meals or by mixing with those rejected by society such as tax collectors and those with no training in the Law. In a way, the "obey-the-rules" approach to religion was straightforward – the key thing was to be obedient to established conventions. In practice, the rules had become so onerous and detailed that almost no-one could keep them except for those who devoted their lives to trying to do so. Jesus rejected this approach and substituted instead a view of man's relation with God on which the Old Testament idea of a Covenant had originally been based. In the last two thousand years, some Christian groups have moved back to the original Jewish pattern that Jesus criticized where the emphasis was on rules and obligations – this is just as much a travesty of what Christianity is about as were the Pharisees' insistence on detailed rules.

The words "freedom" and "love" have been abused and debased so that today it is almost impossible to use them without conjuring up an entirely false impression. Jesus' view of human freedom was a very high one indeed. In all his teaching he considered that human beings had the capacity to break through their conditioning and to respond to God in a direct way, a way that would make a real difference to the world. *The crucial human freedom was the freedom to respond to God – or not as the individual chooses.* If God exists as has been assumed and if God created human beings, then it is not unreasonable to claim that human beings are made for fellowship with God – that is the human *telos*, the human destiny, but it must be freely chosen, it cannot be imposed. The Inquisitor was right to maintain that few people would want to respond in this way, for most the price will be too high. It is important to notice that there is a major difference between saying:

1. Few people will be willing to respond to the challenge which freedom brings.

and

2. Few people are able to respond to the challenge which freedom brings.

(1) is undoubtedly true, but (2) does not follow from (1). (2) rests on an unjustified assumption. Dostoyevsky is careful to have the Grand Inquisitor claim that only the first statement is true while the Inquisitor's whole argument is based on the truth of the second statement. There is no doubt at all that very few people will be willing to take responsibility for their own lives, to live as individuals before God and to live out a relationship with God in lives of self-giving love to those around them. The cost of this is simply too high and the sanctions of misunderstanding, disapproval, scorn, rejection, material loss and isolation which such a path often entails are too high a price to pay. Jesus recognized this clearly. Nowhere did he say that following his way would be popular, it would mean everyone turning against the disciple, even members of his or her own family. Indeed Jesus says:

> "They began one and all to make excuses. The first said: 'I have bought a piece of land and must go and look over it; please accept my apologies.' The second said: 'I have bought five yoke of oxen, and am on my way to try them out, please accept my apologies.' "
>
> (Luke 14:18-19)

> ". . . no man is worthy of me who does not take up his cross and walk in my footsteps."
>
> (Matthew 10:38)

Too often today Christianity is portrayed in childish terms. Christ is presented as "gentle Jesus meek and mild", becoming a Christian is seen to involve no more than going to church, singing a few hymns and being nice to people. Christmas and Easter are family festivals dominated by Easter Eggs and presents with a church service sometimes added. People are surprised when this version of Christianity is considered to be irrelevant to the real world. The vision that is so often presented is an emasculated version of the original, shorn of its radical nature for fear of upsetting people. The resultant bland mixture is not particularly distinctive or appealing. Jesus' call was never bland, it was highly demanding. St Paul recognized (1 Corinthians 13) that when people grow up childish things need to be put away, and this includes a childish understanding of what love, freedom and the fight against evil are about.

The Inquisitor claims, rightly, that most people will not want to follow the narrow, stony and hard path that discipleship involves and therefore, out of love for them, the Church that he represents takes away the possibility. Instead it gives them what they want: bread, mystery and authority. It caters for people's physical needs and their "spiritual" needs are dealt with by "magic" services and a firm authority that tells people what to believe and to do. As the Inquisitor says to Jesus:

> "You pride yourself on your chosen ones, but you have only the chosen ones, while we bring peace to all . . ."

Sometimes peace can be purchased at too high a price and the peace thus bought may be illusory. The people in George Orwell's *1984* had peace, but it was an evil and empty peace. The Psalmist warns against those who say " 'Peace, Peace' when there is no peace" and the Inquisitor's peace is false and illusory.

It is significant that the Inquisitor talks of people "giving up" their freedom, thus assuming that they do have the freedom to respond but want nothing more than to give this up as the price of taking responsibility for their own lives would be too heavy. The Inquisitor's analysis is incorrect because he does not accept that there is a challenge here to which every human being can respond. Indeed the great equality between all human beings, black, brown, white and yellow; male and female; rich and poor; intelligent and unintelligent, is to be found in their joint position as individuals before God. They can choose to respond to God or to turn away. The ability to respond does not depend on outward circumstances but on an inner decision. Every person is, at the end of the day, a single individual, each one may live, learn and work within the community but in the final analysis it is as individuals that people must give account of themselves before God, often standing out against accepted values in the world.

It may be counter-argued that the position is not as simple as this. The freedom of most people may be held to be greatly constrained. The constraints are various – sometimes freedom is regarded exclusively as "freedom to" decide on how to live, but it also needs to be regarded as "freedom from" poverty, oppression, violence, persecution, structural injustice, racism, sexism and many other factors. Most people are not free because of factors that are beyond their control. It is all very well to talk of freedom when writing for those in the affluent First World, but when this idea of freedom is applied to those dying in the Third World the idea may be held to be ludicrous. To say to the young girl on the streets of Lima who is forced into prostitution at the age of eleven; to the young boy in Mozambique forced to kill his friends or be killed himself; to the mother in Ethiopia who watches her first child die of starvation; to the father in Afghanistan as he contemplates the stumps of his legs blown off by a mine left over from the years of war that they are free seems laughable. Those in the First World are, in fact, only apparently better off in the freedom stakes. Many, many people suffer from severe psychological constraints as discussed in the previous chapter. If one takes all the circumstances that affect individual lives into account, then the Christian claim that people are free to respond or not may be argued to be false.

However these counter-arguments fail to recognize the nature of the freedom that the religious demand assumes. It is a freedom that is not based on the individual's calling in life; their material prosperity or indeed outward circumstances. The only true freedom, as Socrates, Plato, Jesus, Kant, Kierkegaard and many others have recognized, is to be found in the inner realm, in that internal freedom which does not depend on external contingencies. This includes the freedom to have power over oneself; to direct one's own life and to be an autonomous agent which is the necessary precondition for being able to love and to be fully human. This freedom can be found in every society and in every part of the world – indeed the poor peasant in Africa or Latin America may have greater internal freedom and integrity than those in the affluent West. This inner freedom is the universal birthright of all human beings, the problem is their reluctance to use it.

Many people may think they are making a free decision when in fact they are not. Following a particular religion may be due largely to background, education and culture. If one is born in Iran, one will grow up to be a Muslim; if in Greece, a member of the Greek Orthodox Church and, in many parts of the South of the United States, a more or less committed evangelical Christian. In most cases religious affiliation owes more to the chance of birth than to any free decision. It is true that some people do convert from one religion to another, but their numbers are small in relation to the many who do not. The followers of the Christianity of the Grand Inquisitor's day were mostly not free. The Inquisitor was right to recognize that they had given up their freedom on the altar of certainty provided by the Church authorities; in so doing they had abdicated their autonomy and their essential humanity.

Being born into a culture does not guarantee that one is genuinely following a particular religious path. There is more to living a life of self-giving love than following laid down rules and rituals. As Søren Kierkegaard clearly recognized (writing under the pseudonym Johannes Climacus in *Concluding Unscientific Postscript*, trans. Hong & Hong, Princeton, 1990), the objective truth of man's relationship to God has to be made subjectively true for each individual so that it is lived out in his or her life. This does not mean, as some existentialist philosophers have held, that each individual must make his or her own truth and live by it authentically. If there is a God and if human beings are made for relationship with him, then this relationship cannot be entered into second hand, it is a relationship on which each individual must embark for him- or herself. Talking about a relationship is one thing, living it is another.

Jesus summed up the whole of the essence of the Jewish Law and the Prophetic tradition in two commandments:

1. You shall love the Lord your God with all your heart and soul and mind, and
2. You shall love your neighbour as yourself.

Indoctrination which seeks to deprive people of freedom undermines the possibility of a free response, yet this is the approach that the Church of the Grand Inquisitor takes and it is for this reason that he rightly recognizes that the Church he represents is in the service of the forces of evil and not of God. The same, it must be said, can and does sometimes happen today.

The Grand Inquisitor's analysis of the human condition is substantially correct. The call to follow God is a call to a life of selfless love, of service to others and to making God the centre of one's life. This means putting all the normal preoccupations of the world into second place. This call will be unpopular and few will be prepared to accept it. The Grand Inquisitor's answer is to give people what they want – and this is where he was wrong. What people want and that of which they are capable are two entirely different things. A child may not want to work, but it is only by learning that she will be able to develop her potential and it may be necessary for her parents to "push" her against her will to apply herself because they realize this is in her own long-term interests. Similarly the Churches' task should be to help individuals to realize their full potential and not to be satisfied with mediocrity.

If human beings are to be free to make themselves into the sort of people they are capable of being, or to reject this possibility, then it is necessary that they be shown that they have the freedom to make choices as these choices will have decisive significance both for themselves and for others. I have already referred to the extent to which the individual's psyche and the world in which we live are dominated by forces that curtail human freedom. These forces, whether or not their origins lie wholly within the human psyche, have acquired enormous power. The fight to bring us back to that freedom of which everyone is capable is a long and difficult one, both for each individual and for the community.

Many modern theologians have abandoned the idea of individuals being called to enter into a relationship with God and have instead developed a wholly incarnational or supposedly Trinitarian theology which sees the whole world as "graced" because of Christ's incarnation. God is to be experienced solely within the world (as Nicholas Lash argues in *Easter in Ordinary*) rather than in the manner that William James (*Varieties of Religious Experience*) envisages. This approach tends to reject what Lash derides as "The Cartesian View" that God somehow exists independently of the world. God is, instead, to be found as mystery wholly within the world. Lash argues against Karl Rahner's understanding of holy mystery. Rahner's view of God as holy mystery represents the God who is ontologically distinct from the world and who is the sole ultimate and absolute mystery but who is nevertheless also immanent within the world – this is a true Trinitarian view. Lash substitutes for this a one-dimensional mystery found only within the world and not in any sense ontologically beyond it. This, however, is a travesty, albeit a subtle travesty.

Certainly it is right to seek and find God in all the day-to-day activities of life, as St Ignatius of Loyola and the Jesuit spiritual tradition clearly recognize, but the God who is thus found is also the God who is ontologically independent of the world as well as immanent in it; it is the God on whom all creation depends and yet who does not depend on creation; it is the God found in private prayer and the God experienced, as William James recognized, in rare moments by the saint and the mystic as well as the ordinary man or woman of faith. This God calls each and every individual equally to a life of love and of service and it is only in finding this life that true freedom will be found – as John's Gospel puts it:

> If you dwell within the revelation I have brought, you shall know the truth and the truth shall make you free.
>
> (8:32)

It is only in relating to God that the forces that seek to constrain and bind humanity, the forces of selfishness and self-concern, the forces of those belief systems which have been inculcated into people, the forces of materialism, pride, arrogance, self-assertion and the like, can finally be left behind. For an individual to discard past certainties and to take responsibility for his or her own life in relationship with God is an unnerving experience. It means each person has to take him- or herself seriously, that he or she can no longer hide in the crowd. Each person has to recognize that actions count and that he or she will be accountable for them.

These will not be popular ideas. They assume that people matter, that each individual is of tremendous worth and has great potential which he or she is capable of realizing. The cost of trying to realize this potential will, however, be high. It is as if one were training for a race – it will be much more comfortable to talk about racing, to watch others race on television or to think of something else than to go out and actually train yourself, to push yourself up against your limits and then beyond them. St Paul likened following God to running in a race and it is a good parallel.

Reference must be made here to the theological idea of grace. Some theologians have held that faith is a gift from God and would maintain that to emphasize human freedom is to wrongly hold that salvation can be earned. However, if God's grace is only given to some chosen people, we have a form of spiritual apartheid at work.

If God exists and if human beings were created for relationship with him, then this relationship is available to everyone – it is a universal and not a selective offer. God does not have favourites. Grace is available universally but individuals have to choose whether or not to respond to this offer. This is where human freedom is decisive, in the decision whether or not to respond to God. The invitation of grace is open to each and every individual but the free response is required to take up the invitation.

The effects of individual past decisions and the decisions of many, many others who have influenced each person are not easily overcome. Original sin does indeed dominate human lives, not in the sense of a sin committed by the mythical figures of Adam and Eve which depict the dependence of the world on God, but the sin and selfishness which are the human legacy everyone inherits and to which everyone constantly contributes. The legacy from the past is so great that it might seem grounds for despair. With these chains around human necks, what hope is there for any real sense of freedom? Christ's claim is that this hope is to be found in God. Christianity is precisely an optimistic religion because of its insistence on the power of hope. Indeed hope for the future is one of the most important parts of the Christian message – the hope of overcoming the legacy of the past; the hope of a new way of living in this world; the hope of a redemption of the world through engagement with it and, also, the hope of individual survival of death.

Human beings can be helped to overcome the effects of their own sinful actions on themselves; to overcome the institutional and societal chains that dominate them and they can be brought to freedom and to truth, but they must want to overcome these obstacles and the chief problem, just as it is the major sin, is human pride. If one's pride and self-sufficiency are such that one refuses to recognize God, that one refuses to recognize one's dependence and one's need, then there is very little that can be done. It was pride that is traditionally held to have led Satan to rebel and it is pride that is the single best insulator between human beings and God. This is one reason why apparent disasters such as illness or a family tragedy can be beneficial as they can force people to recognize their mortality, their frailty and their dependence. When you are fit and healthy and all is going well, then God may seem an irrelevance.

Evil is not simply a matter of the obvious evils of which people are all aware. It is much more far-reaching and complex than that. All those seductive forces that seek to separate people from that of which the human spirit is fully capable may be evil – and the attractiveness of these forces and their beguiling character is their most dangerous aspect.

This understanding also has a radical impact on an appreciation of the nature of forgiveness. Evil tends to perpetuate itself. People have long memories and the hatred of one individual, group or family for another, the enmity between different tribes or racial or national groups, is a costly legacy from the past. Each new generation is educated into the prejudices of their forebears – thus Catholic and Protestant communities in Northern Ireland are brought up to be suspicious of and to dislike each other; Serbs and Croats in Yugoslavia and Czechs and Slovaks in Czechoslovakia have regarded each other with mutual antipathy for hundreds of years; the Basques try to bomb their way to independence from Spain; French Canadians look back several hundred years and want to see their separate identity affirmed in nationhood; the Hispanics of California look with suspicion on their poor black neighbours; the Zulus, the Xhosas and the Ndebele cordially dislike each other in Southern Africa and so the cycle of suspicion and dislike continues. Similarly, the rich nations of the world seek to maintain their stranglehold on a world economic order that favours them and to ensure that the poor nations do not prejudice their enjoyment of their prosperity, thus contributing to structural evil. Almost wherever one looks one finds self-interest, self-preservation and selfishness at work and it is this legacy from the past, perpetuated in the present, that Christianity claims Jesus sought to overturn.

Jesus' answer to the problem was simple. His followers should care for not just each other but their enemy as well. They should absorb evil rather than retaliate. If asked to give their coat, they should give their cloak as well; if compelled to travel one mile they should travel two; if hit on one cheek they should turn the other. This understanding overturns all the normal ways of looking at the world. It rejects all ideas of prejudice and self-interest. Jesus constantly refused to accept the idea that some group was privileged, he cured the Roman centurion's daughter; a tax collector was one of his closest friends; he said that he found more faith in a hated Samaritan woman than in the whole of God's chosen people; his parable of the good Samaritan and the criteria for selection at the Last Judgement both show that ritual and verbal assent to religious propositions are not what is required.

At the end of the day, most evil is due to factors within human control. God paid human beings the compliment of loving them enough to give them freedom and leaving them free to exercise it. C. S. Lewis put it like this:

> If God is love, he is by definition something more than mere kindness. And it appears, from all the records, that though he has often rebuked us and condemned us, he has never regarded us with contempt. He has paid us the incredible compliment of loving us in the deepest, most tragic, most inexorable sense.
>
> (*The Problem of Pain*, chapter 3)

The depth and the tragedy are due to the choices individuals make with the freedom his love has given us. If they deny this freedom, as the Grand Inquisitor thought that most people wanted to do, they are in the end denying not only God but also their own human worth and their potential destiny. The door to evil is then wide open. Individuals are being content with a transitory and low-level happiness represented by their material wants being adequately catered for and greed, pride and self-concern will come to dominate. However, the price for using freedom to respond to others in love will undoubtedly be high, as Lewis again recognizes:

> Love anything and your heart will certainly be wrung and possibly broken. If you want to make sure of keeping it intact, you must give your heart to no-one, not even to an animal. Wrap it up carefully round with hobbies and little luxuries, avoid all entanglements, lock it up safe in the casket or coffin of your own selfishness. But in that casket – safe, dark, motionless, airless – it will change. It will not be broken, it will become unbreakable, irredeemable. The alternative to tragedy, or at least the risk of tragedy, is damnation. The only place outside Heaven where you can be perfectly safe from all the dangers and perturbations of love is Hell.
>
> (*The Four Loves*, chapter 6)

Perhaps Ivan Karamazov and the Grand Inquisitor are right that the price of freedom and the potential for love that it brings is simply too high. Perhaps people would have been happier as automatons, programmed to obedience. Measuring happiness is not easy. It is an old philosophic chestnut to ask who is happier, a pig with his nose in the trough or Socrates discontented. Similarly a human ant-hill of people who are fed, clothed, housed and who enjoy the normal human pleasures is superficially attractive, but perhaps people are made for much more than this.

The reward for responding to God will be opposition, persecution, rejection and suffering – but also, if the path is truly followed to the end, a peace and a joy that can be found nowhere else. "Joy" here does not mean a transitory emotion which can quickly turn to despair. It is, instead, a steady, firm, deep and unvarying assurance that nothing can separate the individual who lives this life from the reality of God. He or she has "come home" in that the purpose and destiny of human life have been found. The fruits of people who follow this path are found in gentleness, in compassion, in understanding, in a lack of self-assertiveness and in love. These fruits are rare indeed, but like a candle in a dark room, they can shine out in the midst of darkness and, in the end, can overturn and overcome any evil forces that range against them.

Summary

The assumptions which the Chrsitian makes can now be expanded by one further point:

– I believe that human beings are made for fellowship with God and it is only in responding to this possibility that true happiness can be found. Human beings are free to take responsibility for themselves as individuals, no matter what their circumstances, and to respond to God or not. I accept that the price for doing this will be high and that the road may be one that few will be willing to follow.

SIXTEEN

Conclusion

The key presupposition of the second half of this book is the existence of God as traditionally conceived and it is right to recognize that if this is rejected then the whole argument collapses. Perhaps this world is meaningless, perhaps the evil that exists is just due to the debased character of human beings as we exist for a few short years of selfishness before fading into oblivion. The first half concluded that Ivan Karamazov's charge that the suffering of innocents is not worth any potential price is persuasive, even if not logically necessary. If reason alone reigns supreme, then the weight of argument may be on Ivan's side. This is not an uncommon view and although modern writers frequently proclaim it, it has a long history. Tolstoy writing in his *Confessions* says:

I remember when I was eleven years old a high school boy named Volodya, now long since dead, came to see us one Sunday and announced the latest discovery made at school. The discovery was that there is no God and that everything we were being taught was pure invention (this was in 1838). I remember my older brothers taking a great interest in this news and even allowing me to join in the discussion. We all, I remember, became very excited and took the news as something very enthralling and entirely possible.

However there is an alternative and it is an altogether more optimistic one. Tolstoy took most of his life to come to the realization of this alternative and it was a painful journey. He saw life as meaningless and, at the age of fifty, in spite of being highly successful on the surface, he constantly thought of suicide. He summed it up this way:

> I realized that despite our intelligence the conclusions of Schopenhauer and myself were foolish . . . if life is meaningless and I am so fond of reason, I must destroy life as the only way I can deny it. All our arguments went round and round in a vicious circle, like a wheel that is not attached to the carriage. I came to realize that the most profound wisdom of man is preserved in the answers given by faith and that I did not have the right to negate them on the grounds of reason and above all it is these answers alone that can provide an answer to life.

Augustine's position, "I believe in order that I may understand", rests on an opening judgement which cannot be proved, but once this is accepted then many things make sense which would not otherwise do so. The faith position is an altogether more positive and optimistic one than the assertion of meaninglessness. It maintains that although evil is a terrible reality it can be overcome and one of our main tasks as human individuals is to fight against it. Indeed the problem of evil is not at heart an intellectual one so much as an existential one – the presence of evil should call us to engage with it and to fight against it. As soon as we are overawed by evil's power and allow it to have mastery we will cower beneath it in fear and trembling. We may have many excuses for doing this, we may hold that it is none of our business, or consider ourselves too weak or think that as we are not too badly affected it does not matter. Evil, however, spreads and unless it is combated its power will grow. We cannot stand idle and watch it increase – we have to face it now no matter how great the personal cost may be. Some may consider us foolish and certainly fighting evil wherever we find it (particularly in ourselves) can be a lonely and heartbreaking business. However the choice is simple: submit and be overcome or stand and fight and find freedom. This is a choice that needs to be lived out and so this book is, at the end of the day, a call to action.

We are now in a position to put together the various assumptions on which the Christian response to the mystery of evil rests. These are as follows:

i) I accept the existence of a creator God as previously defined.

ii) I make a supreme value judgement (chapter 9) by which I hold that the ultimate purpose and meaning for human existence is to be found only in fellowship with and love of God and living out this love in self-giving love to those around us. For this reason I call God good as God is, for me, the ultimate source of everything I value most highly.

iii) I accept that God is Almighty, but by this I do not mean that God is able to exercise total power in the world (chapter 10). God's power is shown in weakness. Nothing can separate me from God's love and because of this God can help me to overcome in every situation even though this may lead to my torture and death.

iv) I believe that God can act in the world in response to the prayers of believers (chapter 11). God cannot, however, be controlled, but he can and does answer prayers. However, such actions by God are going to be rare and sparingly used. We cannot see the possible effects of divine interventions and, in placing our petitions before God, must nevertheless accept that his will should be done as only he can see the implications of any possible action. Prayer therefore involves trust.

v) I am aware of the existence of physical evil and am appalled by the suffering it causes. Nevertheless, although I cannot prove it, I hold that God could not have created a better universe given his ultimate purposes and that we need to see ourselves as a part of the world with a responsibility for it (chapter 12). I maintain this because of the value judgement I make in (ii) above. Because of my belief in and love for this God, I refuse to accept that a world with less suffering due to physical evil could have been created – although I recognize that I am making an assumption here which I cannot justify.

vi) I am in no doubt about the reality and power of the forces of evil lodged deep in the human psyche. I also consider it, at the least, possible that there may be a force of evil ontologically independent of human beings (chapter 14). Even if there is, however, I am sure that this force can do no more than persuade, it cannot take away our ultimate freedom to act. I am convinced that the power of evil is very real and that it needs to be fought both within us and in the world around us.

vii) I believe that human beings are made for fellowship with God and it is only in responding to this possibility that true happiness can be found. Human beings are free to take responsibility for themselves as individuals, no matter what their circumstances, and to respond to God or not. I accept that the price for doing this will be high and that the road may be one that few will be willing to follow.

viii) I accept that I could be wrong about all the above statements but am ready to stake my life on the "if" that I am right. I cannot do more.

This appears to be a long list of assumptions – particularly since good reasons cannot be given for all of them. However, responding to the love of God and becoming a creature transformed by freedom is not a decision that can simply be made by believing there are good reasons for doing so. Religious belief is ultimately a faith relationship with reality itself, it includes a commitment to the belief that whilst the above assumptions may not be rationally justifiable, they are nevertheless right. It is to make a life investment, to stake one's life on an "if". There are no guarantees, merely a history accounted for by believers in a certain way and a knowledge in one's own heart that one has an immense capacity for love as well as the enormous potential of an individual human being to stand against the forces of evil and, in the end, to overcome them.

Peter Vardy is lecturer in Philosophy of Religion at London University's Heythrop College, and is the author of the highly acclaimed *The Puzzle of Ethics, The Puzzle of the Gospels,* and *The Puzzle of God.*